MENTAL & PHYSICAL

FITNESS

SAILING

... & John Whitmore

Fernhurst Books

© Fernhurst Books 1993

First published in 1993 by Fernhurst Books, 33 Grand Parade,
Brighton, East Sussex.

Printed and bound in Great Britain.

A British Library Cataloguing in Publication record for this book is
available from the British Library.

ISBN 0 906754 94 1

Acknowledgements
The authors and publishers would like to thank John Macfadyen,
Director of Physical Training at the University of Southampton, for his
comments on the MS and permission to use the University's facilities
for the photographs; Joanna Buckley for appearing in many of the photographs; and the RYA Racing Division – particularly Jenny and Paula
– for all their help. John Derbyshire would like to acknowledge his debt
to the work of Dr Neil Spurway, John Harrison, Margaret Pashkey,
Anna Nissen and Captain Tim Barrett. His section of the book is dedi-
cated to the memory of the late Gerry Barrel, who devoted a great deal
of his time to developing fitness techniques for sailors.

Photographic credits
All photographs by Julia Claxton, with the exception of those supplied
by the following individuals or agencies:
John Woodward: page 95.
Yachting Photographics: pages 23, 33, 48.

DTP by John Woodward
Diagrams by Jenny Searle
Cover design by Simon Balley
Printed and bound by Ebenezer Baylis & Son, Worcester

Contents ——————————

Introduction

You know the feeling, It's blowing force 6 and you are powering towards the gybe mark. You know you have a good chance of winning the race, if only you can stay upright. And then the rot sets in.

'Now come on, be positive', says the little voice in your head. 'Take the sheet straight out from the boom, get that tiller extension out to leeward. Make sure you are travelling at full speed down a wave before you gybe. Oh no! That gust is going to hit at just the wrong time! Blast! duck when the boom comes over, you idiot! Now straighten up, not too much and… Damn, she's going over, don't let out that sheet…'

From your vantage point clinging to the hull, you watch the fleet sail effortlessly by, gybe smoothly, and hammer off down the reach. 'Told you so', says the little voice.

Brain sailing
We're sure you spend a lot of time and money learning about the technical aspects of sailing. That's fine, but sailing is also about the things you cannot find in technical books: the way the boat feels when it is set up properly, the sound it makes as it moves through the water, the shape of the sails. Learning about these things is usually left to experience – but need not be. This book describes a way to enhance your learning, to escape from the passivity of learning to sail by mere experience.

Mind sailing
Top-flight sailors the world over have discovered the importance of building their confidence, coping with stress and maintaining their concentration. Being able to stay concentrated over a long period is crucial in sailing. It is also important to know how to cope with distractions, and how to refocus when things go awry.

You probably have your own, very personal ways of dealing with these issues, but it is unlikely that you will have stumbled across all the techniques described in this book. Using them may help you find that extra edge.

Body sailing
These days the gains to be made from better mast/hull/sail combinations have dwindled as everyone becomes aware of the current state of the art. Where once you may have been able to conjure up a ten per cent advantage by these means, you will now be struggling for a mere one per cent – the vital ingredient that will enable you to draw clear of the fleet.

You can find that extra in yourself. By building up your endurance, strength, flexibility and speed you can effectively supercharge the systems in your boat – without infringing the class rules!

Psychology and physical fitness
The fact that the topics of psychology and fitness are among the last books to be published in this series gives an indication of the reluctance of sailors to look at themselves – both at their minds and at their bodies. It is far easier to buy new sails, change the centreboard or simply blame a bad shift!

By taking a critical look at yourself using the framework described in this book it may be possible to identify weaknesses and then take the appropriate form of training, whether mental or physical, to reduce or eliminate the weaknesses and create a new strength.

We have enjoyed writing this book. It describes techniques we have found effective for sailors at Olympic level, but there is nothing elitist about the ideas. We hope you enjoy reading about them, and feel motivated to incorporate them in your own mental and physical training programme. Good luck – and good sailing!

PART ONE

BRAIN SAILING

Sailing is one of the most complex sports around – if not the most complex. The mental demands are astonishing. You need an ability to understand and solve complicated problems: your campaign, the regatta, the rules and the technicalities of your boat all come into this category. You also need to develop great subtlety in the way you pick up cues from the boat and its surroundings which enable you to control it on the water.

Psychologists and scientists have discovered that these two very different sorts of mental processes take place in two different, specialised parts of the brain. Technically, these are the left and right cerebral cortices – but left and right brain will do nicely. The left brain is very good at verbal, analytical, sequential and logical tasks, while the right brain specialises in intuitive, creative thinking, deals with wholes rather than parts, and understands spatial relationships well. Obviously these are complementary ways of dealing with the world, and we need both of them to function adequately.

One way to think of these differences is to see the left brain as being good with facts, while the right is good with 'feel'. Since sailing is about both, you might ask how much is it about facts, and how much is it about feel? The answer is that it depends on your craft. If you are a boardsailor, feel is more important; if you sail a Flying Dutchman, the technical aspects figure high on the agenda. But if you want to win races you cannot ignore one in favour of the other: You must develop both, regardless of the type of craft you sail.

This section of the book addresses ways in which you can use all the powers of your brain – both left and right – to improve your sailing. It describes how you can use your logical powers to organise your training and competition sailing. This is known as goalsetting: the most useful and powerful technique available to help analyse your strengths and weaknesses, improve your learning, build your confidence and help you control your stress. It also introduces some very effective techniques which you can use to improve the sort of creative, intuitive sailing which sets the gifted sailor apart from the average sailor. Used well, these techniques can achieve quite stunning results.

Both of these approaches are skills. As you learn to use goalsetting, you will get better at it; and as you learn to use effective self-coaching better, the effects will become apparent. So don't be surprised if, at first, you don't succeed. You wouldn't expect any skill to work on its first, second or even third outing. However, persistence and practice will pay off, as is true of every skill you use in your sailing.

Goals and goalsetting ————————————

Everybody needs a dream: to learn to sail in heavy weather, to win the club championship next year, to compete in the Worlds, to come back from the Olympic Games with a gold medal. These, or something like them, are the ideas that motivate many people to take part in the sport of sailing. Unfortunately, reaching your dream is not quite as simple as buying a fast boat and getting plenty of time on the water. But fortunately, the long job of turning the dream into reality can be helped immeasurably by understanding about goals and learning how to set them for yourself. We have started our book with this topic because it is both a logical and crucial beginning to the process of your development as a high-performing sailor.

Goalsetting is a way of bringing a structure and a discipline to the process of learning. Our experience with sailors at all levels of the sport has been that it is the most important single mental skill which they can master. It speeds the process of skill learning and it is one of the most powerful methods of building and maintaining confidence. It also has a major role to play in helping competitive sailors cope with stress.

Make no mistake, setting goals is a skill, and you will need to invest some time and practice before you will be able to do it properly. This chapter will introduce you to some of the concepts, and suggest a way in which you can use goalsetting for yourself.

DIFFERENT KINDS OF GOALS

How often have you gone on the water with the definite intention of going yachting and winning the race? Or of coming in the top half of the fleet, perhaps? That is one sort of goal, which might be called an *outcome* goal. It is the commonest kind of goal that people use, but unfortunately it has two major drawbacks.

First, you are not in control – the outcome depends on other people's performance as well as your own, not to mention the unpredictables which make sailing such a unique sport.

Second, it is extremely fuzzy. The research evidence is very clear about this second factor. You will stand a much greater chance of achieving a goal if you are able to define it accurately. 'Going yachting' is too general, giving you the option of setting off in all sorts of directions. 'I will be one of the first five boats over the line' is precise, understandable and gives you something to aim for but, unfortunately, even this is out of your direct control. If it were something like 'I will be over the line within five seconds of the gun' it would be a very different sort of goal. This is called a *performance* goal since it specifies quite unambiguously what you actually have to do. 'Get to the weather mark by the fastest and shortest route' is an excellent performance goal; 'get the spinnaker down and stowed inside ten seconds' is another. Of course, there are many more; put them all together, and you may – or may not – achieve the outcome you want. But at least you are in control, and when success comes, it is you, and only you, who have achieved it.

That is why, in many sports, people talk of 'personal bests'. If you can achieve what you set out to achieve, your confidence will grow steadily and inexorably. Building your confidence on the back of other people's performance is, quite frankly, sheer lunacy. That is why performance goals are important.

That said, in sailing it is notoriously difficult to find a way of measuring performance. If you are in a big keelboat, and you have satellite positioning equipment, you can see

1 THE RELATIONSHIP BETWEEN DIFFERENT KINDS OF GOALS

From this diagram, it is clear that various kinds of goals underpin the dream goal. We have found that when top-class sailors learn to stay at the process level, and build success at that level, they gain a solid confidence which cannot be dented by the occasional result which goes against them. You will need that sort of confidence if you are to reach your dream too.

LACK OF CONTROL

DREAM GOALS

OUTCOME GOALS

PERFORMANCE GOALS

PROCESS GOALS

| TECHNICAL | TACTICAL | FITNESS | MENTAL FITNESS | LIFESTYLE |

how fast or how far the boat is travelling. In a dinghy, this is impossible. Often, the best that can be done is to use the moving goalposts of other performers to give you some relative idea of your performance. This is far from ideal.

That is why top sailors use what are called *process* goals. Underlying performance is a whole raft of processes which make that performance happen. The most obvious of these are boathandling skills. Some of these will be technical and some are much more intuitive; the next chapter will go into more detail about this topic. But what about other skills – for example, the mental skills needed to help you cope while you try to handle the boat in adverse conditions and fierce competition? Some of the other chapters in this book will address these ideas. Don't forget fitness, either.

Sailors often talk about 'race fitness'; later in this book you will read about what that really means.

Other kinds of process goal you need to consider are tactical goals. Do you go racing and respond off the cuff, or do you have a clear race plan, and contingency plans? What do you do if you are being caught up on the run? Or if you find yourself in a tight situation at a mark rounding? Rules are one thing, tactical goals are something else. Finally, if you are in the business of mounting a big campaign, you will need to think about *lifestyle* goals – managing the financial side of things, getting sufficient sleep, staying off the booze, eating the right kinds of food, getting your weight right. Unless you pay attention to these aspects of sailing you are not going to be successful, because your international competitors almost certainly *are* paying attention, and using goalsetting to help them achieve success in these areas.

What makes a good goal?

There are good goals and there are bad ones. Knowing how to set a good one can ensure the success of your goalsetting efforts, and that is where the skill of goalsetting comes in. One of the most powerful tools you can use when setting goals is what is called the SMART test. This has been developed from a great deal of research into the properties of effective goals, and is an acronym of the qualities you should build into your goals

S stands for specific. The clearer the goal, the easier it is to see a way to achieve it.

M stands for measurable. If you are to gain confidence from reaching your goal, you need to be able to know that you have achieved it.

2 IMPROVING YOUR GOALSETTING SKILLS

First, bearing in mind that goals need to be challenging, a legitimate question might be 'How challenging?' To get the maximum effect to boost your confidence, you should set goals which you think you have a one-in-three chance of reaching. Those are hard – but if you achieve them you get a really warm glow of satisfaction, and another click on the confidence accumulator. However, that rule only applies to training, not competition. Setting challenging goals effectively puts you under stress, so when you add in the stress of competition, the difficulty rating of goals should come down to a two-in-three chance of achievement to keep the total stress within manageable limits.

You should ask yourself a number of other questions about the goals that you have set yourself. These will ensure, as far as possible, that they conform to the SMART and POSITIVE guidelines. Incidentally, as time goes on, the answers to the questions will also help you improve your goalsetting skills.

First, for each short-term (weekly) goal, answer the following questions as objectively as possible, rating them between 0 (definitely not) to 4 (definitely yes).

1 Does the goal set a specific target?
2 Will it take me towards my medium-term goal?
3 Is this target independent of other people?
4 Can I measure my success?
5 Can I realistically expect to attain it in the time available?
6 Will I be excited and satisfied when I achieve it?

If you score 20 or above, the goal is likely to be a good one. A score of less than 15 means that you should reconsider it, identifying where the major problem lies from your answers.

At the end of the week, evaluate how well you achieved that week's goals. You may need to adjust your medium-term (monthly) goals appropriately. At the end of the month, you may need to reconsider your long-term goals. Try not to tinker with the goals other than at these times, until you have built up sufficient goalsetting expertise.

A is related to achievable. Goals which are too difficult get ditched; but goals which are too easy go the same way. They need to be challenging if you are to think them worthwhile, and get maximum benefit from them. **R** means relevant. It is all too easy to work on your good points, but effective goalsetting demands that you work on your weaknesses.

T is time-phased. You need to think of goals over short, medium and long terms.

Finally, goals need to be POSITIVE. 'Don't capsize' is an example of a negative goal. What was the first thing that came into your head as you read it? 'Keep the boat upright' carries a much more positive image, and one which would be better to adhere to!

THE TIME DIMENSION

For most people, the dream goal is probably a long way ahead. You might, for example, be the best sailor in the club, and fancy your chances at the Olympic Games 12 years hence. You might have just bought a Laser, but actually want to get involved in the Whitbread. Getting there might look virtually impossible – until you start to break down the problem into manageable chunks. Then, by establishing a time-scale, you can identify the crucial stages you will need to have reached in a year, two years, or five years. These are called long-term goals, and will probably be outcome goals.

The problem is that they will seem very remote, and you need to operate over a shorter time-scale if you are to maintain your effort and commitment over such a lengthy period. Usually, you will be looking some three months ahead, setting what are called medium-term goals; these may be performance goals, but may also be process goals. Finally, to get down to the nitty-gritty of training, you need short-term goals. These will certainly be process goals, and operate over a week-long timescale.

There is nothing particularly unique about such a scheme; many people may already be using a similar idea, often in another context such as work or study. The crucial factor that will determine its success, however, is your skill in setting SMART and POSITIVE goals within it. You will find a few hints about how to do this well in Box 2.

WORKING ON YOUR WEAKNESSES

You may recall that, earlier in this chapter, we said that good goalsetting means working on your weaknesses. That can be quite hard to do, unless you have some system which helps. Here is one which we have found effective.

First, you need to make a list of the processes which you think are important for success in sailing your class of boat. Come up with as many as you possibly can – this is a brainstorming exercise, so don't eliminate any *a priori*. To help you get started, here are a few ideas. Some of them you will like, and some you will not. Add any more you can think of.

- Sailing well in light airs
- Heavy weather reaching
- Heavy weather running
- Heavy weather beating
- Coping with shifting conditions
- Sailing through waves
- Gybing
- Short tacking against a current
- Starting well
- Avoiding being PMSed
- Coping with tidal starts
- Coping with biased starting lines
- Mark rounding
- Good windward tactics
- Spinnaker work
- Coping with the crew – or the helm
- Protesting successfully
- Navigation
- Pre-race planning
- Boat tuning
- Present levels of strength
- Present levels of endurance
- Covering duels

- Holding on to a lead
- Sailing in big fleets
- Sailing against international competition
- Sailing against an arch-rival who is always try to out-do you
- Being able to recover from a mistake
- Getting enough training in
- Sailing at night
- Knowing the rules

Now, give each of them a score out of ten, where ten means 'I am absolutely perfect at this'. Then, pick out the eight processes on which you score lowest, and enter them into the outer ring of the 'dartboard' opposite.

Next, indicate their score by a heavy line across that sector; you may want to shade-in the resulting shape. This gives you a personal profile on which you can base a goalsetting programme. Most importantly, it enables you to keep track of changes as they occur, and improve your confidence as well as your skills. If you don't like the dartboard use a histogram, which can be either vertical or horizontal. It really doesn't matter, so long as you can keep track of your goalsetting 'profile'.

3 BLOCKS TO PROGRESS

In two columns, under the headings External and Internal, list all the things you think are standing in your way, leaving a space in the Internal column opposite each of your external obstacles.

Insert the internal component of the external obstacle in this space. For example, you may have 'Lack of money' in your External column; opposite might appear 'My belief that my old boat is not as fast as the others' or 'My unwillingness to work harder or get a better-paid job'.

In your External column you now have a list of obstacles, some of which may seem to be outside your control. However, the corresponding items in the Internal column bring all these problems within your control. There is no denying the external reasons (no one wants to sail a slow boat), but your internal reaction to them may be hindering you more. So let go of those external things that you cannot do anything about and concentrate on the things you *can* do something about – the internal components.

If you have trouble identifying the obstacles, adopt the 'What? When? Where? How much?' technique. You will meet this again in the next chapter. It is a way of sharpening-up your awareness of subconscious focuses.

What is my interference?
When does it occur?
Where does it occur?
How much (on a scale of 1-10) does it interfere?
This should clarify your awareness of your obstacles. 'My anxiety about boatspeed is my interference. I only worry about it on the first lap, and mainly on the first beat. It wrecks me 5/10 on the Richter scale'.

There are many destructive tendencies which are also obstacles. You should be able to find several of these, but to give you an idea of the kind of things to identify, and to jog your memory, here are four obstacles which are very common in sailing.

One is to blame poor speed on the boat. The sad truth is that 90 percent of the time it's you, not the rig or hull. If you don't believe that, get someone you admire to sail your boat. Usually you'll be amazed how fast she goes.

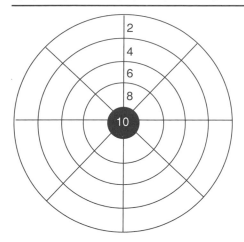

Now, possibly with your coach, you can go on to develop a daily/weekly training schedule which includes working on these skills. At the end of the week, update your 'dartboard', and notice the changes before designing another training schedule.

Finally, everybody has problems with goalsetting. It is best to acknowledge this, and find a way to tackle them. Usually these problems are caused by incorrect application of the SMART test. If this checks out, however, obstacles of one kind or another may be getting in your way. Box 3 describes a way to find out if this is the case, and

Another obstacle is the assumption that the big names are always faster than you. Quite often they are not; they just much more consistent. Check out their championship results: hardly ever does anyone win every race, and anyway, speed isn't the only thing. In fact, speed in the wrong direction puts you even further back!

A third is the inability to resist doing something desperate, or at least inappropriate, to catch up with the leaders. If they are sailing well, you have to settle for the waiting game and just keep sailing at your best. Often they will make a mistake or two which may give you a chance. If they don't, there is nothing you can do anyway.

A fourth is the fear of success. Some people fear winning because of forebodings about what it may lead to. 'If I win the club championship I'll have to go round all the open meetings' or 'I'll have to give up all those hard luck stories which get me so much sympathy and attention'. That sounds like the ultimate 'Poor me'. In fact, if you win the club championship you don't have to do anything. You can retire from sailing if you like, and take up golf.

To eliminate each obstacle may not require great struggle and effort. Accurately identifying it is half the battle. A major advantage of the internal approach to problem solving is that awareness itself is often inherently curative. We are dominated by the obstacles that we are unaware of. We gain control over things of which we are fully conscious. Once a problem is highlighted, it can often cease to be a problem.

You must take responsibility for the internal obstacles to your goals, and for the obstacles that arise on the day.

Let's look at another example to illustrate the point more graphically. Suppose you are going pretty slowly and you reckon the sails are wrong. Your conclusion is that the boat can't win with this rig. You sit back playing 'Poor me'. How could the sailmaker have done this to me! But wait a minute. Who bought those sails? Who hoisted them today? Who is forcing you to use them? And in any case, if Paul Elvstrom were using them, would he be back here? How bad are they really? And what about tactics and strategy? Can't you get up there without raw speed? Wouldn't a better approach be to change the sails when the race is over, and in the meantime get on with the race?

makes some suggestions about ways to deal with possible blocks. Later chapters will deal with these techniques in more detail.

GOALS IN COMPETITION

These days, many top-class sailors go racing with a set of very clear process goals at the front of their minds. For some of them, this comes naturally; they have picked up the techniques and the skills as a 'by-product' of years of experience of sailing at international level. These sailors often find it quite unbelievable that other, less fortunate souls cannot do what they can with such nonchalant ease.

Other sailors have learned how to set and focus on process goals from scratch. They have recognised how having very specific process goals for every leg of the race helps them to stay in touch with what is happening, instead of thinking about generalities.

One crew worked very hard on this aspect of their sailing in the run-up to the 1992 Olympic qualifiers. They had something to think of, and work at, right up to the final mark rounding. But then they abandoned their goals and just tried to beat the other boats in a race to the line. Does this sound familiar?

At first they could not understand why their sailing fell apart on the final beat. When they realised what they were doing, they began to set goals related to the processes which would achieve the fastest possible time up the beat, while not forgetting the tactical goals which are often vitally important at this stage in the race. The results were quite dramatic, and although they failed to qualify they were so motivated by the exercise, and protected from the effects of 'failure', that they immediately vowed to enter the boat for the 1996 Olympics!

So try to think of racing as a series of challenges, each with very specific processes and tactics which underpin your performance. Identify goals for each of these, and you will be well on the way towards a very different mode of sailing in competition. When you use goalsetting in this way, you put yourself very firmly in control of what is going on. This means that every race you enter is an opportunity to be successful. Think what effect that would have on your confidence!

However, the real world always intrudes, especially in sailing. Your race goalsetting plan may come to naught if you find it hard to ignore the possibility of winning, or the presence of other boats, or if the conditions change to those which you dislike. So be prepared to modify your race plan, possibly quite dramatically, if this happens.

Finally, it is worth recognising that goalsetting offers a very valuable way to handle stress. There are two ways in which it can work. The first, described above, is by providing you with a 'game-plan', so that the extra stress of having to think while performing at your optimum is removed. Second, goals can help you stay on top form by giving you something very specific and concrete to think about, rather than worrying thoughts. This technique will be described later in the book in more detail. For now, simply trust that your natural skills can use appropriate process goals to shape the nature of your performance.

Good luck with goalsetting. Its benefits will extend outward from sailing to many other areas of your life. Once you learn to use it properly, you will wonder how you managed to muddle through! Since competitive sailing is getting more and more 'professional', you can no longer expect to muddle through and compete successfully on the international scene. Goalsetting is one sure way to raise the level of your professionalism.

2 Sailing the natural way

Nature has endowed us with some very comprehensive thinking equipment, which has the ability to do several very different things. In the left side of the brain are the circuits which enable us to think logically, understand sequential relationships and communicate with others. However, we also have the ability to be intuitive and creative, and to understand spatial relationships; these faculties are found in the right side of the brain. Of course, we need to be able to do all of these things in our everyday life.

The natural and the conscious mind

The working of the left brain is what we are most aware of, and one way to describe it is to call it our conscious mind. The working of the right brain might be called the natural mind, because it seems that many of the things it does happen very naturally, without involving much thought. For example, just think how a child learns to walk. He sees others doing it and plays around with walking until he finds the way that works best for him. It comes naturally, and it's effective: no-one has walking lessons, and yet everyone learns to walk pretty well.

You may have experienced the power of the natural mind yourself. 'Going with the flow' and 'Getting in the groove' are phrases which describe what it feels like to do things with your natural mind. When you sail at your best, it probably feels quite natural and effortless because you don't have to think about it. The natural mind doesn't think – it leaves that to the conscious mind. Of course sailing effortlessly is not all there is to competitive sailing. You also need to think tactically and logically, communicate with the crew and so on. In fact the fascination of sailing is that you need to use *all* your mental faculties to make a decent job of it. You need both the powers of the natural mind and the abilities of the conscious mind – indeed there is probably no other sport

which is quite so demanding. The ideal surely must be to let these two brain modes operate independently, and as required.

Two points need to be made about the ideal. First, the natural mind needs to be able to sail automatically, so that you don't have to think about sailing – because having to think means that the conscious mind is trying to do it! Learning to sail automatically is just the same as learning to walk automatically: you simply do lots of practice until you can do it. The problem for most people is that although they practised walking every day as often as they needed to, they probably only work on their sailing skills for a few weekends a year. So it would be very useful indeed to make this limited experience as productive as possible.

Second, the conscious mind and the natural mind are always engaged in a battle for control, and it is usually the conscious mind which wins (see Box 1). It knows, you see, and tends to be a bit big-headed about all this knowledge. The problem is that it knows facts and theory, not procedures. The difference between these might be called 'knowing what' and 'knowing how'. Only the natural mind has the capacity to learn how to sail. You need strategies to stop the know-all conscious mind from interfering with the natural mind as it does this.

The rest of this chapter is about ways which may help you achieve automatic, natural learning when you are training. A later chapter will explore in more detail what happens when the conscious mind runs riot.

IMPROVING – NATURALLY

People are natural learners, and learning is a process that never stops. You learn about yourself and the world you live in, and you learn about how to operate in that world. Natural learning is like building up a huge mental filing system of your experiences, and having a very good index which enables you to locate all these experiences almost instantaneously. Having done this you can compare what you did on previous occasions with the current situation to help you decide what to do. All this happens unconsciously, automatically, in your natural mind.

Many coaches and textbooks will offer you factual 'what to do' knowledge, and much of this information is very useful indeed. But these facts are not the same as 'how to do it' knowledge, and this you cannot get from instruction or books. Your natural mind operates with this procedural, 'how to do it' knowledge. Quite often, of course, you can turn 'what to do' facts into 'how to do it' learning as you put advice into practice. So by all means give it a go.

You will probably find that the most physically comfortable way of doing things is also the most efficient, and that this coincides with the textbook method. However, because everyone is constructed slightly differently, sailing styles also differ slightly from person to person. So as you try to interpret the experts' words you need to take account of the differences between your body and theirs, the differences between the boats, and probably the differences in the helms and crews you sail with. Try out their ideas and find out what works for you, and under what circumstances.

If you work this way, you will learn from your own experience, rather than from the words of the experts. Your natural mind will have learnt how to sail, while your conscious mind, quite incidentally, will learn about the facts of sailing.

Diverting the conscious mind

At first, when you are picking up a new skill, the conscious mind seems to be very busy trying to work things out and telling you what to do. It is trying to take over from the natural mind, and unfortunately slowing up the process of natural learning. But how can you prevent this, and divert the conscious mind from its habitual interference? One approach might be to encourage it to get involved in the process of learning by giving it something to do which would naturally be helpful: you could ask it to focus on the task of collecting information to put into the filing system in the natural mind. The conscious mind knows all about awareness, so why not use it!

Awareness is simply the experience of what is going on here and now. It does not consist of ideas, judgements, opinions, analyses, fears, criticism, complaints, and thoughts about what should or ought to be going on. Unfortunately the conscious mind is very good at generating all these. The trick is to stop it offering up all these interfering thoughts, and encourage it to deliver

1 THE BATTLE WITHIN

Most of us, at one time or another, have heard the little voice in the head saying things like 'Do it like this: Put your left hand – oh no, not like that, stupid. Can't you do anything right?' or even 'You might as well give up now – you'll never be any good.' Recognise it? Who is talking to whom? Obviously one part of you which doesn't trust another part very much. That is the battle between your conscious mind and your natural mind. As well as being a critic, your conscious mind can make you anxious or destroy your self-confidence, so performing and learning take a back seat. But that is a story for later chapters.

experiences as vividly as possible. These come through the senses: the feel of the tiller in your hand, the wind on your face, the tightness of your muscles as you pull on the sheet, the sound it makes as it moves through the water. If you can get your conscious mind to stay with these experiences, it is working for you and not against you.

By getting your conscious mind to concentrate on the widest possible range of experiences, you are turbo-charging your natural learning, not putting the brakes on.

RAISING YOUR AWARENESS

You can go way beyond the facts of sailing by directing your attention to your sensory experiences as you practise the experts' suggestions, instead of letting their suggestions rule your life. The key to doing this is to ask yourself questions about your experiences as they happen.

The most important question is 'What is happening?' To answer this, you will need to call on all your senses: Sight, hearing, touch, balance and, very importantly, the feeling within your own body. In other words, you must really attend to the sensory experiences which your natural mind needs to work from if it is to learn. As far as you can, try to simply attend to this raw, pure information. Don't pollute it with criticisms, opinions or analyses. Your natural mind will process it very effectively without conscious interference. Trust it. Remember that's how you learned to walk. The one question to avoid is 'Why did that happen?' Since this means you are back in the past, and being logical instead of natural. It's easy advice to give – but it is very hard to implement!

From the 'What is happening?' question you can go on to others which enrich the data your natural mind needs in order to learn. Other powerful awareness-raising questions are 'Where does it happen?', 'When does it happen?' and, most powerful of all, 'How much of it is there?'. These questions force you to categorise your experience in various different ways, to cross-index it – and to learn from it.

When you ask the 'How much' question, you should use some sort of scale to refine your experience, such as how much heel there is, how much pull there is on the tiller, or how quiet the boat is downwind. More often than not, you will have to use a subjective 1-to-10 scale for this, and that seems to work very well. You may need to stretch it a bit when you get to eight or nine out of ten: eight point one, eight point two and so on. The reason for the scaling is that the better the quality of your awareness, the better your learning will be, and using a scale means that you avoid answers like 'not much' or 'a bit'. Your natural mind is like a computer – put garbage in, and you get garbage out. So aim to put the clearest, most accurate information into its files! Box 2 has some tips which may help you to do this in new ways.

'But I'm always aware of what's going on', you may snort. Yes, you probably are, but everyone can go deeper and deeper into their experience and reap the benefits. Improving your awareness can have the effect of causing a correction to your skill to happen quite subconsciously in your natural mind. For example, suppose you enhance your awareness by being more descriptive: instead of saying 'My arm hurts', try 'My wrist is twisted to the left, and lower arm muscle burns when I pull on the sheet'. This locates the problem accurately, describes it and gives the natural mind some idea of what to do about it. The chances are that the pain will subside.

EXPERIMENTING

Sailing performance is about adapting constantly to changes in the wind and water conditions. It goes without saying that if you have sailed in lots of different conditions, and have used a variety of settings in practice, you are likely to be more sensitive to what is needed under those conditions, and if you get the settings wrong, at least you will be better able to cope with the problem. For this reason many sailors deliberately experiment with conditions and settings.

Unfortunately it can be all too easy to find one good way to do something and believe it to be the only way. That is a recipe for unnecessarily limiting your potential. Remember: the more information you can store in your natural mind, the more effective and flexible your performance is going to be on the day. So devise as many ways as you can to give yourself wide-ranging experiences. Get out of the rut – experiment! Box 3 should help you start the process.

To get the best out of experimentation, don't forget to keep your awareness raised

2 IMPROVE YOUR SENSORY EXPERIENCE

Sailing is a very sensory sport. You need input from virtually all your spatial senses to perform well. So when you are asking yourself 'What do I notice?', take account of every sense. If you find this hard to do, take a tip from some coaches who advocate blocking out some senses to enhance others. For example, closing your eyes will increase your sensitivity to hearing and touch. If you focus on the sounds alone when beating to windward, your hull speed will tend to increase but you will probably come off the wind. Conversely if you block your hearing, you will depend even more on sight than usual, with the effect that you end up sailing so close to the wind that you lose boatspeed. Experimenting with this will show you how you gather information and which sense to use for a particular effect. The sense that we neglect most is feel. Because it is neglected, its potential is the least developed, which makes it our most valuable sense for improvement. Close your eyes and block your hearing at the same time, and you will be obliged to depend on the feel of the tiller. You may be surprised how well you can sail. You are likely to maximise the combined efficiency of speed and direction. Your over-compensating tiller movements will reduce by half. Now you will know how to balance out the use of all your senses to the best overall effect.

The focused attention evoked by these exercises is every bit as important as the specifics of the particular exercise. Each exercise occupies your conscious mind as an information gatherer, allowing your natural mind the freedom to get on with sailing the boat. That is the way you learned to walk, look how well you do that!

Here are a few more ideas about seeing, feeling and listening to things as you practise. Try them, and see if they help you.

Heel
Sail hard on the wind on one tack for several minutes. Every few seconds rate your heel on a scale of 0 to 10: 0 for upright and 10 for the masthead hitting the water. Say the scores out loud if it helps: 'Two, two, one, three...' Don't try and aim for a score or keep the scores constant; just concentrate on recording as accurately as possible what the heel is. You are heightening your consciousness, maximising the filing away of experience, letting your body be absorbed in the way the boat feels at various angles of heel, and probably having more fun on a long beat than you thought possible. You may also find you are sailing fast; don't force this, but trust your natural mind's ability to process the accurate information it is receiving and move you automatically towards your goal of greater speed to windward.

by asking the right questions as you sail. Remember that experimentation is not just going yachting; it's about adopting a sensible, structured approach, and that's where goalsetting comes in.

Spend some time figuring out which bits of sailing are controlled by the conscious mind, and which bits are controlled by the natural mind. here are a few ideas to start with, thought up by some Olympic sailors. There are sure to be more, think up some for yourself, or with your crew.

Conscious mind skills
- Wind and tide directions relative to the start-line.
- Position relative to other competitors.
- Compass headings.

Telltales
Beat for a while watching the telltales near the jib luff. Don't *try* to keep them streaming; just observe them continuously and let the helm correct itself (as your awareness increases, this will happen automatically).

The compass
Now watch the compass as you beat. Sing out the readings over a period: '120, 125, 130, 125, 130 ...' Then try it on a run, keeping the boat at the best angle to the wind.

Waves
On a beat, reach or run say: 'trough, crest, trough, crest...' at the *exact* moment that the bow reaches them.

Mainsheet traveller
When beating, keep your hand lightly on the tiller and steer with the traveller. Note the position of the slider relative to the centre point, and say: 'up 10cm down 4, up 20...'

The tiller
Still on a beat, concentrate on the feel of your hand where it meets the tiller. Rate on some self-devised scale how hard your're pulling the helm and stay with it for as long as it interests you.

Tacking
Rate yourself on a 1-10 scale for 'speed across the boat' and 'effortlessness' on a series of tacks.

Downwind sailing
Use a scale such as 'floatiness'. See if you can notice it getting better with practice. Don't try too hard to *make* it happen, though – just *let* it happen.

Listening
Listen to the sound of the bow cutting through the water. Can you hear the bow hit each wave crest? Listen to the silence between the crests. What does it sound like in a trough? Is there a difference as you luff and bear away? Can you hear the boat speed up or slow down? What happens to the sound as she heels?

3 EXPERIMENTATION

Here are a few more exercises you might try to help you break out of the mould.

- Try tacking on lifts instead of headers
- Swap crews with another boat
- Try racing in another class
- Swap sails
- Rake the mast aft
- Change roles within the boat
- Swap roles. Give a different person the authority for strategy, tactics or tuning.
- Spend the last half-hour before the race in a different way
- Try a different way of deciding where to start
- Alter your final approach to the startline – take a longer or shorter run at it.
- Deliberately change your attitude. First, describe yourself as a sailor in one word such as 'cautious'. Next, decide on the opposite: 'bold'. Try sailing the next race as if you were bold. At each stage imagine what a bold sailor would do next – then do it!
- Try to devise an exercise for your pet weakness. You may worry a lot about manoeuvring before the start in the melee of boats. Try looking at the water *between* the boats rather than at all those hulls. (In fact this makes more sense, because we usually go where we're looking.) Your nervousness will evaporate, because there *is* room. You can see the possibilities, not the problems.

- Favoured side of the course.
- Check systems for spinnaker hoist.
- Bearings to the marks.
- Rig settings.
- Wind and wave conditions.
- Course changes.
- Nearest end of finish line.
- Control of fleet.
- Tactical decisions.

Intuitive mind skills
- How the fleet will behave.
- Judgement of start.
- Steering the boat through the tiller.
- Feel of the boat in the water.
- Feel of wind pressure.
- How low to trapeze.
- How hard to turn the boat.
- When to come off the trapeze.
- Feel of the waves.
- Balance of the boat.

- Flatness of the boat.
- Crew position fore and aft.
- Angle to sail the boat relative to the wind on the run.
- Crew and helm movements in the boat.

The goal-setting dart-board can be used for both these categories of skills. Draw a vertical line down the middle of the board, so that the conscious mind skills are on the left, and the natural mind skills are on the right. Now you have a technique for setting and measuring two very different sorts of training goals.

You may be wondering how you measure abstract ideas like the feel of the waves or the shape of a sail. The easiest way is to think of a word which describes it to you. The word can be as daft as you like, so long as it captures the essence of the experience. Then, by using the ten-point scale, you quantify it. For instance, words to describe the feeling of tacking might be effortless, or controlled, or aggressive; the feel of the boat downwind might be flat, or quiet. It is absolutely vital that you use your own word, because your perception of what is happening is unique to you.

If you and your partner on the boat want to improve the way you sail together, try having the helm ask the crew what the boat feels like when you sail it in a particular way. Can he or she feel that? When, and how much? By doing this you are building up a powerful shared perception of sailing together, and developing a language that enable you to talk to each other about it.

STAYING IN THE WINDOW

One of the temptations when training is to try too hard. You wouldn't be human if you didn't push yourself, but you may be surprised to know that the natural mind doesn't learn well when you are trying to concentrate too hard. Sailing with raised awareness does not mean that you are tensing up and studying the jib luff with furrowed brow, and trying to get it spot on. It is quite the reverse. You should aim to be in a state of relaxed concentration.

This means staying in the here-and-now, observing clearly what is happening. Olympic sailors call this sailing 'in the window': a time window which has no history and extends only a short time into the future. If you are not in the window, you are not sailing the boat, nor are you learning from your experience.

How big is this window, you may ask? When several world-class sailors were asked what was going through their minds as they approached the gybe mark while racing in really hairy conditions, most reported that they were thinking ahead, to the position they wanted to be in ten or 20 boat lengths past the mark. So long as they stayed in touch with what was actually going on in their window, they trusted that

their natural ability would take care of the sailing.

This meant trusting their bodies to reproduce the best of all they had learned and experienced. It meant trusting that, by being totally aware of what was happening, they would automatically and effortlessly give the best performance they were capable of in the conditions. Sure, these sailors were trying; they were trying with every sinew and ounce of strength and agility they possessed. But they had learned to leave the sailing to the natural mind, by achieving a state of relaxed concentration.

Unfortunately, the conscious mind is very quick to offer criticism while you are learning to sail better. It thinks it knows what to do – which may or may not be true. This conscious, critical function can stop the natural mind getting on with the serious business of learning how to sail better, simply because it is all too easy to listen to thiscriticism instead of staying 'in the window'.

For example, 'I wouldn't pull my cunningham on as hard as he does, because I might go slower' is a typically unhelpful comment from the conscious, critical mind. The truth is that you learn something new every time you carry out an activity in a different way. What's more, finding out what doesn't work is just as valuable as finding out what does work. Maybe you will go slower with a tight cunningham, but at least you've proved it for sure. How about having it slacker than usual? If that doesn't work either, you will now really know for certain where the boundaries are, and can stop speculating – which is what the conscious mind is so prone to.

The golden rule is: don't let your conscious mind get in the way of natural learning. It is yours to control, so use it to gather accurate information which the natural mind can insert in its files. Don't let it be vague, and don't let it put in 'That's wrong or bad'. Use the 'what', 'where', 'when' and 'how much' questions, give yourself lots of varied experiences, and *stay in the window*.

PART TWO
MIND SAILING

Elite sports performers employ a number of mental strategies to help them use their physical skills and abilities to the full. Some of these mental skills are concerned with preparation for competition, and some are concerned with firefighting on the day. Both are important if you are to get the best out of yourself in competition.

The skills for preparation include:

● Mental rehearsal, including using imagery during deep relaxation.

● Detailed planning of both the strategies and tactics of competition.

● Effective goalsetting to build confidence.

The skills they use for firefighting are:

● Concentration control, enabling them to maintain concentration at a high level, to handle distractions and re-focus on the task if concentration is lost.

● Monitoring tenseness so that it stays at an optimum level.

● Maintaining confidence during competition through control, and developing recovery strategies in case it should drop.

You may be using some of these mental techniques already, possibly without really thinking about it, or because of something you have read in the past. Good, but if this is all new to you, don't worry. Think of mental skills as tools to help you cope with different types of situations as they crop up. Top-flight sailors from many countries are using them – certainly the Canadians, Americans, British, French, Germans and Irish all have psychologists working with their international sailors. Our own research with the UK Laser fleet has shown that mental skills are very important indeed; 'mental fitness' was a good predictor of sailing form on the top half of the Laser Ladder.

But don't imagine it is only the very best sailors who benefit from mental skills. A moment's thought will convince you that only minor differences exist in boatspeed, handling and rig at any level of competition. It wouldn't be much of a competition if people were not closely matched on these factors. Because sailing is such a complex and demanding sport, the use of effective mental skills offers one way in which you can find an extra edge, whatever your status.

The following chapters should contain something useful for you. Enough theory has been included to help you begin to understand how your mind works, and thus appreciate why the techniques work as they do. These are the very techniques which high-performing sailors on the international competitive circuit use.

However, a word of caution is appropriate. It concerns the fact that most of these techniques are mental skills. Like other skills these can be easy to describe, but time-consuming to learn. Take piano-playing, for example; all you have to do is hit the black and white notes in the right order, and the music comes out of the back of the box. That's knowing *what* to do, but knowing *how* you do it is a very different kind of knowledge, which cannot be found in books. It can only be built up from experience.

So, if you decide that mental techniques may help, you must think of them as just another range of skills which you will need to find time to practise. You would not expect boat handling skills to work on their first outing and, like boat handling skills, mental skills are prone to break down under pressure unless they are well over-learned. The good news is that you can practise them at any time of day or night, in all weathers, and they can often be learned quite quickly.

Eventually, your mental skills will operate automatically and virtually unconsciously. If you talk to very experienced sailors who say that this mindsailing stuff is obvious, or that they never do that, you should treat their comments with a healthy scepticism. They wouldn't be in the position they are today if they had not, somehow, learned excellent mental skills which now operate so slickly that they are unaware of them.

But you can learn them too. Approach the task carefully, using good goalsetting, and plan sensibly. Commit yourself to 15 minutes a day for a month or two, scheduled for the time just before you go to bed, and in a few short weeks you will have almost certainly mastered the major skills.

Finally in this section we have included a chapter on a subject which many people find extremely difficult – sailing together. Most of the interpersonal problems within the cauldron of a racing boat have a large mental component, so the way to tackle them is to use mental skills. Our experience over two Olympic campaigns leads us to believe that when the mix is right on the boat, performance improves automatically. Hopefully you will find some ideas in this section to help fix your mix.

1 WHY BOTHER?

How many factors do you think affect your sailing performance? Five, maybe six? Things like boat handling skills, fitness, tuning, psychological fitness, the gear you use, or how well you get on with your crew or helm immediately spring to mind. There may be a few more too: see if you can come up with at least one more.

Write them down in order of importance. When you have ranked them like this, estimate the weight of each factor as a percentage of the total. You might think that having good gear is worth 50 per cent, your handling skills are worth 25 per cent and so on. Make sure that the total adds up to 100 per cent.

Draw a circle and turn your figures into a pie-chart. The width of each slice of the pie represents the weight of the factors you have identified. You now have a graphic representation of how you value the various factors in your sailing.

Now draw a second circle, but this time make a pie-chart which represents the amount of time and effort you put into getting these factors right. You may be somewhat surprised to see what this shows, particularly in respect of the psychological slice.

Do you think it might be worth doing something about it?

1 The effects of stress ————————

This book is in three sections, but in reality it is almost impossible to separate the workings of the brain, mind and body. This is particularly true when we look at the effects of competitive sailing. Racing puts sailors under stress – indeed you could define sport as an activity which places people under intense physical and mental stress to see who cracks last. This chapter may help you to understand something about stress, how people react to it, and why the various stress-management techniques work.

WHAT IS STRESS?

Everyone knows the word stress, but few people have a clear idea what it is. Here is an excellent definition: *Stress is any demand which is made on the mental or physical capacities of a person.*

You will see that stress is therefore 'out there' in the form of a demand, but it is also 'in here' in the sense that your personal capacities are involved. The crucial question is, can you increase your ability to deal with the demands of competitive sailing by increasing your mental capacity? The answer to this, for almost everyone, is yes.

Everyone is familiar with the effects of stress; both the physical symptoms and the mental consequences. Strictly, these effects are quite separate, but they often happen together and may even interact. They are the products of two very different systems which evolved thousands of years ago to protect us in times of high demand. When stress occurs these systems become aroused, or activated, and we respond to the demand in predictable ways.

Let's look at the physical system. The dry mouth, the sweaty palms, the deep breathing, the evacuation of all sorts of bodily contents – all are the effects of adrenalin. This means that the body is getting ready to do

something pretty violent: either run away or stand and fight. That was a very sensible thing to do when the world was full of sabre-toothed tigers; fight or flight were good life-preserving options. Not so good, though, in the late twentieth century, particularly if you are sitting in your boat helming. If you were a runner you would need, even welcome, these physical symptoms of a readiness to perform well. On a boat, however, they can be a nuisance; these basic reactions get in the way of calm, smooth sailing.

The mental repercussions of demand are slightly more complex. The most familiar one is anxiety: the emotional alarm bell that says 'Get out of here!' This can be triggered by two things. The first is noticing that you are developing a physical fight or flight response; you naturally conclude that there is something to worry about, so you'd better get anxious and leave. Sometimes physical reactions can become conditioned to certain events, just like Pavlov's dogs which salivated to the sound of a bell. You can get het up and anxious in this way over anything: the sight of your deadly rival, the sound of the ten-minute gun or even the smell of the exhaust from the rescue boat. This linking of physical arousal to danger cues was a very sensible mechanism in the jungle, but it tends to be a problem in sport. It can be very hard to break these links, and it is often easier to get rid of the anxiety about the arousal.

You can also make yourself anxious by thinking about things. This is the province of the conscious mind. We have evolved a very crafty system which enables us to both avoid dangers and take advantage of opportunities – it is called foresight. By trying to predict possible futures, we have become a very successful species. The problem is that we tend to predict ghastly futures. That is sensible, too. Thinking that the world is a bed of roses is much more risky than assuming it is a very thorny place indeed, and that it is worth taking appropriate avoiding action instead of blundering towards an early, spiky end.

However, it is not quite as simple as that. As well as using foresight, we use hindsight. We size up the known or imagined future demand, and run a check on our capacity to meet that demand, based on our recollection of previous successes and failures. If our perceived capacity seems insufficient to meet the demand, we experience anxiety. If it appears to exceed the demand, we feel confident. So anxiety and confidence are the emotional 'stop/go' signals that we use to help us thread our way through life's obstacles.

This gives us a clue about ways to deal better with anxiety, and improve our confidence. You will have noticed that the words 'imagined', 'perceived' 'appears' and so on were liberally sprinkled through the above explanation. This is because confidence and anxiety are all generated by the conscious mind. Stop it thinking, or change the way it thinks about the world and yourself, and you are well on the way to managing your confidence and anxiety.

One further topic needs to be explored: the relationship between arousal and performance. Very recent work has shown that once arousal goes over a certain threshold, performance suffers a catastrophic slump; recovery takes some time, being delayed until arousal drops very substantially. The importance of this is that the control of arousal is much more critical than was once thought.

Both mental and physical arousal need to be maintained at their optimum for good performance. They need to be high, but not too high. Getting them there and keeping them there demand skills which are controlled by feedback, or awareness. The best performers are very self-aware, and they use this awareness of, say, their level of tension to help them manipulate and control arousal levels to their best advantage. Throughout this book we suggest that you improve your awareness of mental or physical feelings. Without awareness, you cannot have control – and having control of yourself is just as critical as having control of the boat.

Some of the remaining chapters in this section describe a range of ways in which you can gain that control, particularly of mental arousal levels. If you are the sort of sailor who finds it difficult to stay calm under pressure, read on.

2 Managing anxiety

It would be a very brash sailor indeed who claimed that he or she was never anxious. Life-preserving anxiety is a good thing. When it comes to competition, however, anxiety can be a real problem. What happens is that your insistent, conscious mind distracts you from the business of sailing by filling your head with worries. It makes your body tense up so you cannot sail with any degree of fluidity and that unpleasant emotion of anxiety takes all the fun out of sailing.

Let's look at three possible sources of anxiety. First, there may be worries about issues which have no relevance to sailing at all. Things like finance; school, college or work issues; a difficult personal relationship. Sailing has nothing to do with these dilemmas, but your mind can all too often take you back to them when you least want it to. You really need to be able to leave such problems behind when you race in the boat.

Second, there are things that happen on the water. It might be the mere presence of other competitors, or it may be a power boat churning through the middle of the fleet. Do you sail better when your deadliest rival is in the fleet, or do you go to pieces? Top sailors are able to deal with these sorts of problems without getting wound up or anxious.

Finally, the stresses of competitive racing are not confined to the course itself. There is often much 'unfinished business' left over for when you come ashore. The problem is that although emotions can be suppressed and repressed, they will eventually leak out, and can affect your ability to perform at your best in the next race.

So what can be done? Luckily, there are various techniques to deal with anxiety which you can learn to use at various times. Some are of general value; these should be carefully chosen on an individual basis. The ones described in this chapter can work well, but remember that they do need practice. They are based on getting some con- trol over your conscious mind – and that won't happen overnight.

In principle the techniques are simple. Either you divert your thoughts to non- threatening things, or you persuade yourself that either the situation isn't so bad after all, or that you are actually much more capable than you thought. Some methods seem to work well for some people, other methods work well for others.

OFF-WATER PROBLEMS

The four strategies described below range from some very simple and well-tried methods to a surprisingly effective visualisation technique. Choose one that you think you could take to, and build it into your race preparation procedures.

Time management A surprising amount of anxiety is generated by thinking about chaos, and the difficulties of dealing with it in the time available. The easiest way to cope with a complex job, especially one with emotional demands, is to get it organised on paper. Once it's there, and not in your head, the size and complexity of the problem somehow seems more manageable. In the 1992 Olympics every British competitor was issued with a time management system.

However, you may suffer from worries which are not be of a concrete nature, or which cannot be dealt with before a race. For these you will need to use another technique. The general idea is to parcel them up out of the way, so that you can get on with the job of sailing as fast as you can. Two methods sailors have found effective are the black box technique, and making sure that if you are going to worry, do it well!

The black box technique For this you need to be reasonably good at visualising.

First, find a quiet place, and relax as best you can. Then imagine yourself walking into a room; see the wallpaper, carpet and curtains in colour; look out of the window at the trees and the clouds in the blue sky. Now notice the desk; it has a friendly, old-fashioned look to it, and a chair to sit on in front of it. On the top of the desk is a sheet of paper, and a pen.

See yourself walk over to the desk, pull out the chair and sit down. Pick up the pen, and write your problem on the paper. Feel the pen writing, hear it moving across the paper, read the words you write. Then fold the paper in two and open the drawer in the desk – it's bottom left, double size – and find the box in it. The box is black. Is it wooden, or is metal? Take it out, and place it on the desk. The drawer on the top right has a key in it. Open the drawer, take out the key and unlock the box. Place the folded paper in the box and relock it. Now put the key back in the top drawer and close it. Put the box in the bottom drawer and close that. Get up from the desk, leave the room and close the door. Your problems will remain in the box, in the desk, in the room until you come back and go through the sequence to retrieve the paper and read it.

This you MUST do, at a time you agree with yourself will be appropriate. The problem will wait safely in the box until the race is over. Remember to imagine as many aspects of the room as you can, colours, sounds, smells, feel of the pen writing, the key turning, AND DON'T FORGET TO RETURN TO YOUR LOCKED-UP PROBLEM AFTERWARDS.

The worry period Spend ten minutes each day at a particular time, perhaps after your evening meal, getting all your worrying done. Then you don't need to do it on the water! A piece of paper to organise your worries so that you get the maximum benefit from the period is useful. Try a flow diagram, so that you can eliminate wildly improbable extrapolations into the future. That, after all, is what worrying is – an ability to construct possible futures, so we are prepared for one of them.

There is absolutely nothing wrong with that, but if you are to worry effectively, you must make certain you follow your train of thought to a logical conclusion. Most worriers stop at a catastrophic point, and fail to ask themselves questions like 'Then what happens? And after that? And what is the absolute worst possible result? And *then* what would I do?'. You will find that most worries are quite illogical if you make them submit to such relentless probing.

Mental hygiene Finally, it goes without saying that you shouldn't carry mental garbage into the race. Do whatever you need to do ahead of time to have a clear mind when the racing starts. This might entail writing your will before setting off on the Fastnet, wiggling the pintles to check that the rudder is going to stay put, or climbing the mast to check for cracks.

Routines are good, too. Are you an early or late riser? Do you like to take a leisurely breakfast and get to the boat in good time, or does it all happen with a rush? It might be worth thinking this aspect of your sailing through. For example, some very good sailors like to get on the water early, to feel that it is 'virginal' and more importantly, *theirs*; others like to sail the first beat before the race, checking windshifts, currents and rig settings. The main thing is to feel happy that you've done all you need to do, and that you are ready for the hassles of racing.

DURING THE RACE

The only source of anxiety is your conscious mind, voicing its concern about the demands which racing is placing on you. Logically, you have two ways to gain control of your anxiety. The first is to use your conscious mind to flood yourself with information, so that it simply hasn't got time to worry. This is the basis of the natural sailing method you will have read about in Part

One. Not only do you stop being anxious, but your sailing will improve. This is a very effective method, and relatively easy to learn, but you may find that you need to deliberately shift your attention back to sailing.

The second method is to train your conscious mind to think more sensible thoughts – to become skilful at thinking these instead of the ones which are causing you anxiety. This method also works well, but demands that you practise your new thinking until it is thoroughly grooved in. This section describes both methods in some detail.

Two ways to shift your attention

Centering This Eastern martial arts technique is quick, simple and surprisingly effective. It is useful in lots of circumstances. Basically, you have to try to lower your belly-button by half a centimetre as you breathe out. Try it now, and notice the physical and mental effects as you do so.

1 STRAIGHT THINKING

Do you recognise any of the following in your own thought processes and their associated self-talk? They are all examples of distorted and limiting thought processes. Some of the suggestions for ways to change them may be helpful for you – but remember, you may be trying to change the thinking habits of half a lifetime. That is going to take time and effort, but stick at it until you feel the benefit is permanent.

All-or-nothing thinking Perhaps you tend to see things in black and white categories, so that less than perfection is a failure. Try using a subjective one-to-ten scale to measure your performance, to stretch the black and white into more realistic shades of grey.

Over-generalisation By using the words 'always' or 'never' in your self-talk, you are telling yourself that single mistakes are really a never-ending spiral of failure. Substitute 'occasionally', or 'now-and-again'.

Filtering Have you a tendency to focus on a single negative detail, or a word of criticism? Try writing down all the positive aspects of yourself and your performance to put things into perspective.

Discounting the positive Do you tell yourself that anyone could have done as well when you have a good race? Nonsense! You are a unique human being with a unique history which especially enables you to sail as well as you do.

Jumping to conclusions In the complete absence of evidence, many people tend to interpret things negatively. For example, catastrophising (thinking things will turn out badly) or mind-reading (imagining that people are thinking badly of you). Learn to suppress these sorts of thinking when you become aware of it, by a self-instruction to focus on sailing the boat.

Two things happen. You are forced to attend to a neutral stimulus – your navel – and centering produced a degree of physical relaxation, particularly in your shoulders. Practise doing it in time with three slow breaths. Soon you will be able to do in one breath, enabling you to regain control of your thoughts within a second.

What you do next is crucial. You must get back 'in the window'. Many top sailors have clear process goals for every part of the course; these are ways of recalling the sensory cues they need to think about. So after centering, say to yourself something like 'get back to smoothness!' Then you can begin to rate how smooth your sailing is using the ten-point scale. That should plug you back into natural sailing again, and stall the conscious mind's efforts to make you feel anxious.

Thought-stopping Thought-stopping is another powerful way to control negative or anxiety-producing thoughts. It involves

Magnification Exaggeration of your shortcomings, or problems – or minimising your good qualities – is also a common and debilitating fault. Try deliberately doing the opposite, on paper.

Emotional reasoning By assuming that your emotional reaction to less than perfect performance in some way reflects on yourself, you may be unnecessarily handicapping yourself ('I feel disappointed – therefore I must be a rotten sailor'). You are not your behaviour, and you have a right, like anyone else, to the odd off-day. Put that on paper too, stick it on the wall, and read it until it seems so obvious that you cannot imagine how anyone could believe the opposite.

Self-blame Do you hold yourself personally responsible for events that are not entirely under your control? This is not very sensible; it's the downside of megalomania. Remind yourself – again on paper – that you have a right to make mistakes, and that you really cannot control everything.

Labelling An extreme form of all-or-nothing thinking. Instead of thinking you made a mistake – or two – it's all too easy to think 'I'm a loser'. Try listing your successes, in every area of your life. Use your history to your own best advantage.

It is important for you to monitor your self-talk, understand it and use it to your advantage, just as you would with a physical skills. But a word of caution. Self-talk which is not truly reflective of your thoughts and beliefs about your capabilities, or the challenges which face you, is not credible. Nor is there much mileage in over-inflating your self-beliefs. Getting your thinking straight means just that. Becoming aware of negative self-talk and distorted thinking strategies, and putting them right, will help you reach the limits of your potential. The power of thought is important – but it won't win you a medal unless you actually have the ability to sail well enough!

learning to use words or images to block unwanted mental activity in your conscious mind. You can use the word 'Stop', a red traffic light, or a combination such as a neon sign saying STOP! Focus on this, instead of the obsessive chains of mental rubbish in your head. The word 'Stop' simply jams up your conscious mind. However, it will return to anxiety-raising thoughts unless you instruct it otherwise, so you also need to take a second step after thought-stopping.

For example, you may be feeling tired. Use thought-stopping to take your thoughts off pillows, sheets and duvets, and replace them with empowering thoughts such as 'fight!', or whatever word or image makes you feel wideawake and full of energy.

Or maybe you've been hiking all day, and saying to yourself 'I can't stand this much longer.' Try this technique. Ask yourself 'How bad would the pain have to be, on the one-to-ten scale, for me to actually stop sailing, to demand that I get on the coach boat and go ashore? Nine? OK, that really is the bottom line. Now, how bad is it at the moment? Seven? So, loads more to go. Seven point one, seven point two...' This technique usually works very well indeed.

Both centering and thought-stopping are good techniques to use in real-time, acutely stressful situations. They can be learned easily, too. Try them out in bed when you want to get to sleep, when your mind is wandering in a meeting, or whenever you have an opportunity to practise them.

Self-talk: the conscious mind at work

Almost always, the thoughts of the conscious mind are in the form of self-talk, the term psychologists use for that almost incessant chit-chat in your head. It is surprising that many people are unaware of this until it is pointed out to them. This is probably because self-talk is often so well practised that it becomes almost automatic, and slips out of the front of their consciousness. However, it is certainly having its effects.

To add to the confusion, the conscious mind is not very good at thinking logically.

We all have faults in our thinking which distort our understanding of things, although it is sometimes hard to see this. We get so used to thinking this way that alternatives seem ridiculous. The way to deal with such distorted, anxiety-provoking thoughts from your conscious mind is to recognise them for what they are, and deliberately train your mind to come up with more useful thoughts.

In broad terms, the conscious mind likes to talk about two things: the situation you are in, and your own abilities. When you set about changing your thoughts for better ones, you need to examine each of these categories.

Thinking positively about yourself

It is all too easy to be negative about your abilities. 'I'm no good in light airs'; 'I can't cope with big waves'; 'My starts are lousy, because I might PMS'. Do any of these sound familiar? They are actual examples of statements which international sailors were making to themselves before they undertook to change them.

When you see someone else's negative statements, it is easy to understand the effect they can have. But it is much more difficult to appreciate the effect of what you say to yourself through your own anxiety. Think what the effect would be if someone else said it to you!

When you become aware of negative self-statements, you are well on the way to replacing them with *self-affirmations.* These are simple, positive and direct statements of your abilities. They should not be qualified; no 'quite goods' or 'not too bads'. Take the 'I might PMS' statement. It was replaced with 'I never PMS'; this also happened to be true. Changing 'I'm no good' to 'I like sailing' transformed one sailor's light-air performance dramatically.

You can also develop self-talk strategies which will help you to cope as the stress becomes progressively more acute. These are called *mastery statements*, because you use them to remind yourself that you are a coper, not a wimp.

2 THE TYRANNY OF PERFECTION

When you are looking at your self-statements, it is important to look out for three little words: Should, ought and must. If these occur in your self-statements, you are really making life uncomfortable for yourself. These are evidence of perfectionism – called 'musterbating' in the trade – the irrational and damaging belief that you absolutely must achieve your self-set goal.

A moment's thought will convince you that the whole idea of 'perfection' is nonsense, since the goals you set yourself are always changeable. Although that may be easy to understand, it's not always easy to stop musterbating ...

The cure is simple. Instead of telling yourself 'I must win', learn to tell yourself 'I will do my best'. You will then have achieved two things. By using a performance goal instead of an outcome goal, you have given yourself control; and the word 'will' energises, rather than pressurises. Both ways, you win.

Initially, use statements such as 'I can deal with this situation, no problem', or statements which direct you to cope effectively, such as 'Think of the ways in which you can deal with this'. Then, as the stress increases, use the statements which enable you to confront and deal with intense stimulation as it occurs. These could be 'Just concentrate on sailing' or 'OK, you're feeling tense, this is a cue to take a few deep breaths and centre'. Finally, when the situation is really critical, statements such as 'Right, there are lots of things you can do; keep it under control for a start', or 'Keep cool, this will soon pass' will be valuable. The golden rule is to make up your own credible statements.

Thinking positively about the situation

While it is certainly important to remind yourself that you are a good sailor, it is equally vital to think positively about conditions, race standings, other competitors and so on. The underlying principle here is to change possible threats into challenges. But before you can even begin to do this, you are probably going to need to become aware of the content of your thinking.

The way to do this is to quite deliberately monitor your thoughts. Because these thoughts tend to be rather repetitive and 'skilled', your conscious knowledge of them if often low. Box 3 (overleaf) describes a technique which may help you raise your awareness. By identifying what it is you think about, focus on, and feel like at various stages when you are racing, you may find out something very interesting. You will certainly be a lot clearer about those negative statements about the race – or yourself – which your conscious mind throws up with monotonous regularity. Then all you have to do is change them!

Learning new thoughts

Changing well-practised thought patterns for more effective ones is actually fairly easy to do. When you want to change the way your conscious mind works, the rule is that you need to practise new thoughts until they are automatic. Otherwise, in the heat of competition, the old, well-practised thoughts will surface. You therefore need to commit some time to learning the new thinking skill. This is a two-stage process.

Step one is to write down your new thoughts verbatim, one at a time, on pieces of paper which you put all over the place – on the bathroom mirror, on the steering wheel of the car, on the telephone, and so

3 RAISING YOUR AWARENESS

It can be very helpful to review your thoughts and feelings about your best-ever race and your worst-ever race. Then you can compare one with the other. For some people with excellent memories, this is an easy task. If you cannot remember previous races in that sort of detail, do this exercise just after you have a really good race, and then after a lousy one – or vice versa.

You will need to include what happened on land as well as on the water, and before the racing starts. Make a list of 'mileposts'; these might be in the boat park, sailing out to the course, at the ten minute gun, in the fleet just before the start, at the start, on the first beat, at each mark rounding, on the reaches and the run, on the last beat, and coming up to the finish.

At each milepost, try to record what you were thinking about yourself, the opposition, the conditions, and so on; whether your attention was on the boat, your tactics, the results, or other competitors; and how you felt – confident, anxious, optimistic or depressed. Ask yourself how you should be thinking and feeling, and what you should be attending to. You will have then produced a blueprint for your very own mental skills training programme!

on. This makes sure you read them as many times a day as possible. Quite soon that whole exercise will seem pointless, because you will have internalised these ways of thinking and the notes will have no 'shock value'. At that point you can begin to feel fairly certain that the phrases you have learnt are well grooved in.

The second step uses mental rehearsal techniques. This is covered in much more detail in Part 2, Chapter 5, *Imagery and mental rehearsal*, and you should read about it there. In brief, though, you should come up with a range of situations in which the new thoughts would be useful, and imagine saying them to yourself while mentally rehearsing your sailing. When you get into the real world, the new thoughts are more likely to 'pop up'.

AFTER THE RACE

If you are very uptight when you come off the water, you can burn off the excess adrenalin by going for a jog, cycle or swim. However, this only deals with the physiological arousal, not the psychological component. If you are very angry or upset about someone's actions on the water, and cannot get it out of your head, you could try a technique from Gestalt therapy. This involves focused physical expression of your feelings – but you really need some privacy to do it properly.

Find a soft and yielding object, such as a pillow, kneel down with it in front of you and beat it to death with your fists. You can yell at it, too. Imagine that it is the person you are feeling angry with, and keep it up till you feel peaceful. It sounds daft, but it works very well, and it is MUCH better than off-loading your anger and tension onto your partner in the boat. Not that you would dream of doing that, of course! (see Part 2, Chapter 7, *Sailing together*).

Of course, like many sailors, you may like to use alcohol to change your perception of reality. Psychologists call that maladaptive emotion-focused coping (!) and it works quite well in the short term. Don't overdo it, though!

3 Building and maintaining confidence

Just about everyone would agree that sailing performance and how you feel about yourself are closely linked. If you want to sail at your best, you need to be able to draw on your self-confidence in much the same way as you draw on your boat handling skills, you need to build your self-confidence, you need to maintain it, and you need to ensure that it is as robust as possible. This is called confidence management.

Poor confidence management can affect people's sailing in several, sometimes unexpected ways. For example, many people have an idea of themselves as average to reasonably good. Being *really* good violates this firmly-held belief, so rather than change how they think, most people will perform according to their expectations. Others may believe that they have a personal performance ceiling. This implies that if they reach it, it's all downhill from there on. These people suffer from 'fear of success'. If you ever feel like this, read on. The techniques work well: of all the things which Olympic-class sailors did during recent campaigns, deliberate self-confidence enhancement was the most dramatically successful.

WHAT IS SELF-CONFIDENCE?

Self-confidence arises from judgements you make about yourself. Sometimes you may feel you are a wholly competent person; at other times you may feel so useless that you want to curl up and hide. The process going on when you feel like this about yourself is quite easy to understand.

Everybody's head contains two sets of mental 'tapes', which contain the sum of all

1 PERFORMANCE, MOOD AND SELF-CONFIDENCE

Sailing performance is affected by two major factors: Skill and mood. If your skill is well developed and you feel 'in the mood' you will probably sail well, but sometimes you may feel in a much less positive frame of mind and your sailing performance suffers. Because sailing is a sport where consistency counts for so much, it is important to try to stabilise your mood.

For most people, mood depends quite crucially on self-confidence. For example, adopting the notion that 'I'm no good at helming' or 'I have no sense of balance' creates a mood of pessimism, and such people are very likely to give up, say, Laser or boardsailing. Can you detect any similar thoughts in your own head?

The problem is made worse if you use your sailing performance itself to generate a positive mood. This is quite the wrong way to go about things, but very common indeed. How do you feel when you've sailed over the opposition, or everyone has capsized except you? You probably sail better for a couple of races, and then the effect wears off. Or worse, you get arrogant, lose your friends and stop improving. As always, realism is the key. An accurate and aware self-perception is the ideal.

The trick is to maintain a positive mood which will enhance your sailing. But if you use your performance to generate self-confidence, how are you to maintain those good feelings? This chapter describes how.

you have learnt about:
- What constitutes a 'perfect' person
- What sort of person *you* are.

These 'tapes' are called your ideal self and your current self-image. Your ideal self comprises the sum of your beliefs, rules about behaviour, and sets of attitudes derived from your family and society at large; your current self-image is built up of memories about things that you did well or badly, and things that people (especially you!) told you about yourself.

When you compare one with the other, you generate something between a positive glow (not much difference between current self-image and ideal self), or a feeling or worthlessness (a big difference between them). So the whole process is based on recalling and comparing memories, some of them quite recent.

For example, you may feel great if you have just sailed well, or lousy if you have bombed out. This is because these facts get recorded and read out of your current self-image tape as 'I'm a successful sailor', or 'I never seem to get in the top fifty'. This is interesting, because if you can feel better or worse about yourself as a result of very recently stored positive or negative memories, it suggests that making sure that your taped data is updated positively may have the same effect. And it works, with a little effort.

STAYING SELF-CONFIDENT

Research has shown that athletes who have a high level of self-confidence are more successful at their sport than those who are not

2 CONTROLLED ARROGANCE

Logically, sailors and other performers who want to excel should have such high self-confidence that the occasional poor performance cannot seriously damage it. One Olympic contender described this as 'controlled arrogance'. But if you try to do this you will encounter an insidious problem, since there is a powerful rule in our society that says you are not allowed to be big-headed. Parents, teachers, friends and colleagues are all very good at reminding us about this. The facts are that this rule:
- is confined to this society
- affects women more than men
- is nothing more and nothing less than an arbitrary rule
- can be completely and categorically ignored as far as top-class sport is concerned.

Managing your self-confidence in the pursuit of sporting excellence is not being bigheaded, nor will it make you bigheaded. It is common sense, and is possibly one of the most important things you can do.

It has been done before. The great boxer, Muhammed Ali, used to say 'I am the greatest!' This violated the terribly British rule about not being an egotist, and initially made just about everybody in the UK feel uncomfortable and negative about him. But it made him believe that he really was the greatest, not 'quite a good boxer, Harry', and he became the world-class sportsman that he told himself he was. Eventually, his performances convinced everyone else too.

In a nutshell, he took responsibility for his own mental preparation, and ignored an arbitrary rule which might have prevented this. If you are going to be a top-flight sailor you, too, will need to take that responsibility.

confident. More importantly, they seem to have spontaneously discovered some ways of managing their self-confidence. Other, less successful performers probably start off with a lower level of self-confidence, and find that poor performances seem to pull them down in a spiral of diminishing self-confidence, deteriorating performance, and thus even lower confidence. If this sounds like you, then you must learn how to build up your confidence, keeping it relatively independent of sailing success or failure. The chances are that your sailing will benefit.

SO WHAT NEEDS TO BE DONE?

It's all very logical, really. You change the nature of the information stored in the tapes. Since it is difficult to change the 'ideal self' tape, most sport psychologists will help a performer work on the self-image tape. There are several ways of doing this.

Set effective goals
This first method is the most powerful, and you have already encountered it in Part 1, Chapter 1. Setting effective training and competition goals ensures that the tape records a steady stream of success in meeting challenging situations. Research – and common sense – tells us that success leads to the 'feel good' factor which breeds more success. So the first rule of confidence management is to learn to use goals appropriately.

Immerse yourself in images of success
The second approach is to keep good company, and surround yourself with images of successful sailors. Being close to good performers seems to rub off in some way. Psychologists call this vicarious experience; they also refer to visualizing in this way, so as well as being a way of getting in some dry-land training, visualisation of success has an important role to play in the management of confidence. Part 2, Chapter 7 goes into this in much greater detail.

Re-write the tape completely
There are a number of ways of doing this. Try to:
● Monitor and change all negative self-statements. If you think you are having little chats with yourself which could erode a sense of super-confidence, STOP IT. Listen

very carefully for the self-talk which floods your tapes with 'hear-say'. If you are forever telling yourself you hate sailing in heavy weather, what are you putting on the tape, for goodness sake?

● List all your positive attributes. This means ALL the things you like about yourself, all your strengths, assets and positive qualities. Get help from your partner if you need to. Write them down on a big piece of paper, stick it on the wall, and read it daily. This will have the effect of overwriting any things you are not too happy with, and the tape will soon read out as totally positive – at least for the first few crucial seconds.

● List and keep updated ALL your successes. This is the same sort of thing, but you should list the achievements you have reason to be proud of: scholastic, musical, professional, sporting, the lot. The tape will then tell you that you are really successful at everything you do. The list can also act as an *aide-memoire* for you to use when you visualise. Seeing yourself as successful will remind you, again and again, just how capable you actually are.

● Construct personal affirmation statements. It is imperative to overwrite negative beliefs about yourself, because they get repeated again and again in your self-talk. The first step is to become aware of any negative ideas you may have about yourself, and then counter them vigorously with an appropriate self-affirmation statement. These are most effective if they are written down, with your name included, and used like an antibiotic by taking one of them at a time frequently for a few days until you notice the effect. The statements should be written, read and inwardly said in all three persons, because the source of the original programme is unknown – self, other, or overheard. Incidentally, this works well during relaxation.

These suggestions may sound stupid, but they're logical, and they work. Many Olympic sailors who said they lacked the confidence to sail at their limit were enabled to do so by using these techniques. If you use them, they may give you the extra self-confidence to draw on when you need it most.

3 SELF-IMAGE REPROGRAMMING

There are two things to remember when you consider changing how you think about yourself. The first is that you have learnt every one of the facts about what you are, or have been in the past. These facts are yours to keep; all you are going to do is reorganise them. The system tends to play back the most recent recordings – that is, the first part of the tape. The last part is still there, if you wait long enough; it won't be lost. You are not cheating; you have not changed in any fundamental way. You have just used your unique history in the most effective way possible.

Second, memory does not work quite like a tape recorder. When you try to reorganise your facts, the existing ordering may not be completely erased unless you keep rewriting the new list many times. So you will need to practise your new thinking.

However, you are going to meet resistance from yourself as you do this. The negative images and thoughts are often so well recorded that you can feel quite odd, even giggly, when you state, visualise or read positive ones. Accept this, understand that it is a perfectly normal effect which proves you must overwrite the negatives, and keep going until you feel no further resistance or discomfort about being positive about yourself. At that point, you believe it!

4 Relaxing and energising ─────────

One of the most useful mental skills which you could ever learn is the ability to relax. When your mind and body are relaxed, they are in a state which is quite opposite to that associated with anxiety. Putting yourself into deep relaxation can, in itself, counter the effects of stress, both long-term and acute. And when you are relaxed your conscious mind and your body send fewer and fewer messages which can interfere with imagery. So relaxation is a way of getting the maximum benefit from mental rehearsal.

Relaxing into an altered state of consciousness is a skill, but you can learn it quite quickly. Once you have acquired the skill, it can be honed to perfection through practice. For example, while most techniques of relaxing require you to spend about 20 minutes in a quiet, comfortable place to start with, eventually you can learn to relax for just a moment or two. This can be invaluable in helping you control the arousal which leads, say, to intense anger and shouting at the crew. A couple of breaths, and everything can be sweetness and light again. You can also learn to relax only certain parts of your body which is very useful if you have to give your arm a breather after a long tack, or your legs a chance to recover if you've been hiking for too long.

Relaxation often leads to sleep; that is why Eastern meditators sit in uncomfortable positions, or lie on beds of nails. They don't want to drop off! But if nothing else, relaxation can help you get off to sleep before a big race. Its main use, however, is to set you up for mental rehearsal. If you are serious about using imagery and mental rehearsal to improve your sailing, you must first learn how to relax properly.

There are many ways of achieving a state of relaxation. You probably know of some of these: meditation, yoga, and the progressive muscular relaxation method (PMR) where you tense up groups of muscles and then relax them. There are others, too, such as visual methods, autogenic training and biofeedback. In fact every one of these techniques has the same effect. So why are they so many? Simply because different techniques suit different people. You need to find one that suits *you*.

Usually, relaxation techniques are categorised as body-to-mind or mind-to-body. By relaxing the body, the effect spreads to the mind, and vice versa. Body-to-mind techniques include PMR and bio-feedback, where an electronic device picks up physical measures of tension and translates them into some visual or auditory display. In both cases the object is to make the body relax; bio-feedback simply helps to make the relaxation more obvious, and learning is easier.

Mind-to-body methods are subdivided into two types: Left and right brain techniques. Remember the struggle between the right and left brain? If you have a powerful left brain, you will need to use a relaxation technique which helps it to relax; conversely, if you are a right-brain sort of person, you will need a right-brain relaxation technique. Actually, you may need both; you will have to experiment to find out what sort of person you are, and what suits you.

Some left-brain, conscious-mind methods use a mantra. This works by clogging up left-brain functioning, so that it gets bored and starts to relax. A mantra is simply a word; an Eastern meditation technique uses 'Ommm', but this sounds ridiculous to most people. You can use any word, so long as it is neutral; it's no use using 'Fire!'. Counting sheep works well; many relaxation tapes ask you to count breaths, or say 'Relax' at the end of a long exhalation. However, the conscious mind also *sees* things, so imagery – such as the sheep – may be important if you are more of a visual than a verbal person. Many sailors seem to be; sailing is a very visual sport, and attracts people with the ability to see nuances in the sea or sails which would escape others. Left-brain imagery-based relaxation methods need to be sequential; walking endlessly down a darkening staircase into the gloom is one example.

The right brain deals with patterns and wholes; music is like this, and many relaxation tapes use music to help calm the right brain. But it has to be slow, quiet music – heavy rock won't do. A tempo that works well is one beat per second; this is characteristic of a lot of Baroque music. If you find this sort of music difficult to relate to, there are now many tapes of 'New Age' music which work just as well. And don't believe all that stuff about it slowing your heart-rate down to 60 beats per minute – many top athletes have resting heart-rates of less than this, yet they still find slow music relaxing! Finally, you can now get tapes of relaxing sounds, such as rain, waves on the beach, or trees in the forest. These complex holistic sounds also block right-brain activity, and can help left-brain imagery to become really vivid.

By now you will have realised that many of these techniques for producing deep relaxation are not at all unusual. When you learn to relax, you are simply taking the process to its logical conclusion, and learning to use it to your advantage.

LEARN TO RELAX

Almost everyone can learn to relax quite quickly. The biggest single problem for beginners is that thoughts keep intruding. The received wisdom is that you should adopt a passive attitude and let these thoughts pass through and away, but this is often easier said than done. You will probably find that using the thought-stopping technique will be helpful in blocking intrusive thoughts. The good news is that, eventually, the problem goes away.

Learning to relax is like developing a habit. We all cultivate the habit of being uptight; you can cultivate the habit of being laid-back, too. But first you must begin to notice what the first habit is doing to you; you have to become more aware of the levels of tension which are common for you.

Try leaving reminders around which will help you get into the habit of noticing your tension levels for a few moments. These reminders can be on your watch, on the telephone or on the bathroom mirror. Try to do this at least twice a day, and rate your tension level on a 1-10 scale.

Then you need to practise your relaxation skills. Many people say that they cannot find the time for this. Rubbish! The best time to practise is just before you go to bed; everybody can spare 15 minutes then, and you may find it helps you drift off. Once you have established the skill, you can always find a few moments during the day to consolidate and tune it. Here are some situations we all find ourselves stuck in:
● waiting at red lights
● in a lift
● being put on hold on the telephone
● queuing for coffee or lunch
● when commercials come on the TV
● the first three rings of the telephone

These are good times to take a minute – or even a few seconds – to notice your tension levels and have a go at bringing them down. Relaxing like this will soon become a way of life. You will find that if you say 'Relax' every time you have a go, simply repeating the word will do the trick.

Good luck with your relaxation skills. They are fun to learn, and once you have experienced true deep relaxation, you will use it more and more in many areas of your life.

ENERGISING – HOW TO UN-RELAX

Considering the difficulty many people have with relaxation, the problem of getting the level of arousal up to its optimum after a two

1 IMAGERY-BASED RELAXATION

Lie down somewhere quiet, and relax by whatever method you can. If you haven't done this before don't worry; it's really quite easy. Just attend, in turn, to each foot, leg, hand, arm, your stomach, chest, and back muscles, and try to make them slack. Next, focus a lot of attention on your jaw, forehead, and tongue. When these are nice and floppy, you can start visualising.

The first technique involves thinking of a pleasurable but largely passive state such as sunbathing, or lying on your back in a field or a forest clearing in summer. Think of all the sounds, colours and smells, and the details of the foliage, the sky, the insects and birds. The more vivid your image, the better.

The second method is similar, and involves imagining yourself in a safe place. This can be somewhere from your childhood, a hideaway or favourite chair, perhaps; it may be more recent. It's up to you to find an image which makes you feel completely calm, safe and unthreatened. You should try to hold these images for five to ten minutes, and don't be surprised if you drop off.

Finally, if you find you really cannot sleep, the old sheep trick still works, or you could try imagining yourself being full of a solvent which dissolves tension. As it drains slowly away through little holes at the ends of your fingers and toes, all the tenseness goes with it. This is particularly effective if you suffer from heart-burn or indigestion as a result of competition anxiety.

The nice thing about imagery-based relaxation is that you can do it anywhere. So if you are getting a bit gripped up before you go on the water, find a corner of the boat park and retreat to your safe place. Nobody will know you are there!

or three hour wait for the start in light airs is surprisingly common.

The methods which you might try are fairly straightforward, in that they are the opposite of those which cause relaxation. Probably the most powerful way to energise yourself is to use mental rehearsal which links some trigger to any arousing feeling such as anger, hatred or strength. This trigger can be an image of an appropriate predatory animal, such as a tiger; a remembered shot from a movie (lots of gratuitous violence is quite permissable); a 'mood word' which elicits excitement, such as Kill! Smash! Explode! or Go! or a musical theme related to appropriate imagery, either imaginary or from a film. Some Olympic sailors used *Chariots of Fire* played on a Walkman for the purpose.

Ideally, your trigger will be associated with your feelings at the start of a race. A small physical movement, such as clenching your fist or touching your thumb and forefinger together, can also be built into your rehearsal. When you are imagining your feelings, trigger words and images, you should make this little movement too. Repeating it on the water can help to summon up your energy.

Another method worth trying is to use self-talk to remind yourself why you are where you are; what it means to you; how much effort you've put in already; and that you really want to succeed. And remember that activation is the name of this particular game, so move! Get lots of muscle tension increases, if necessary by isometric contractions, and breathe faster. In effect, you do anything which is the opposite of deep relaxation.

5 Imagery and mental rehearsal

Have you ever found yourself lying awake, unable to sleep, before an important race? Don't worry; thinking about the race the night before is not being neurotic, and it can be very useful if you do it right. In imagining your skill you are, in a way, practising it. OK, it doesn't actually physically happen, but research has shown very clearly that mental rehearsal is the next best thing to physical practice – what's more it's cheap, and you can do it anywhere!

You may feel you are not very good at imagining things, but the ability to use imagery is a mental skill, and as you practise, it will get better. As it gets better its effects will begin to show through. So even if your imaging ability is limited at the moment, you should try to use it as much as you can. Mental rehearsal, through imagery, can also help with confidence problems, as well as lead to improvements in actual sailing performance.

Top performers in many sports regard imagery and mental rehearsal as integral to their training, not something which gets tagged on as an afterthought. However, they start off with simple techniques and gradually work up to the more complex kinds of imagery. This chapter describes some of the uses to which you can put both simple and more sophisticated imagery.

IMPROVING YOUR IMAGERY SKILL

Research tells us that some people can form images more easily than others; some people can form very clear images, sometimes in colour; some people see smooth motion rather than a series of snapshots; and some people see themselves as actors in their images (first-party), while others see themselves as spectators (third-party). The image may be purely visual, may have 'feel' or touch components, or may involve sound. Emotions may also come into it. So peoples' imaging ability is very variable. Luckily, however, most people can learn to produce images of quite high quality if they apply themselves.

If you want to get better at imagery, you need to learn how to produce images which

1 THE POWER OF IMAGERY

Try this party trick, which relies on imagery for its success. Challenge someone, of about your height and build, to a test of strength. This involves him holding an arm out horizontally, palm uppermost; his task is to 'try really hard to prevent you bending it'. You grasp the wrist, place a hand on his biceps, and ask him if he is ready. Then apply steady pressure to bend the forearm upwards from the elbow. Don't jerk it. You will usually be able to shift it somewhat, if not completely.

Now reverse the roles, but this time don't try to resist. Instead, come prepared with a clear image of something which is unbendable, such as an iron bar or a concrete post. When he asks you if you are ready, just concentrate on keeping that image as vivid as you can; closing your eyes helps. He will almost certainly be unable to have the slightest effect on your arm.

are as vivid as possible, with lots of detail. Next you need to develop good control over them – it's no good if they run out of control into scenarios which you don't want to be in. And third, you need to be able to use both first and third-party imagery at will. Box 2 gives a few exercises which should help to develop and strengthen your imagery skills.

2 IMAGERY EXERCISES

Here are a few exercises to help you improve your command of imagery.

Vividness
Imagine you are in the boat park, all alone. Notice how quiet and lonely it is, and pick out all the details. What can you see? Boats, covers, trolleys, gear? What colours are the covers, which classes of boats can you identify and what are they standing on? What can you hear? Is it windy? What is the state of the water, and the sky?

Now it's different – full of competitors, spectators and supporters. Tune into the bustle, the noise, the sight of others. You are getting ready to go on the water. What do you feel? Tense, excited, annoyed, calm? Who are you talking to – what are they wearing?

Then you are on the water. Hold that tiller and mainsheet in your hands – or perhaps the jibsheet and trapeze. See those tools of your trade in great detail: their texture, colour, temperature, wetness, smell. Now use them well: feel the skill within you, the sounds the boat makes as you do so, the pull of the sheet in your hand. Run the image again and again, picking up as much detail as you can.

Controllability
Pick a skill you do well – tacking, perhaps, or hoisting the spinnaker. Imagine doing it, in as much detail as you can: the sights, sounds, feel and smell. Speed it up, and slow it down. Do it in practice, and do it in competition. What emotions did you notice in each case? Good and bad? Try it again with the good emotion.

Now repeat the exercise with a skill you are not so happy with. Recreate the situations where it goes wrong. Slow it down until you can really feel where it breaks down, and now do it right, again and again and again.

First and third party imagery
Think back to a situation where you sailed well. Use all your senses to recreate this, as if you were actually there. Notice those emotions, the feel of your body movements, and what your attention was on. Now imagine flying up into the air and landing in the rescue boat. From there you can see yourself, still sailing, as others see you. Notice how you are sitting or hiking, the way the boat is behaving as you sail it, and how the other competitors are being affected by your skilful sailing. Doesn't that make you feel more confident?

These are just ideas. Imagery is all about the power of imagination, so come up with a few more imaginary situations which you can use to improve the vividness, controllability and nature of the imagery you have at your command.

FAMILIAR USES FOR IMAGERY

The most common use of imagery is in the mental rehearsal of skills. It can be used both to learn new skills and to improve existing ones. For example, before the season really gets going you can use mental rehearsal techniques to improve your boat handling skills. Lots of imagined runs of a particular skill, in slow-motion if you can, will add to your 'experience' of that skill being performed. Think of imagery as 'building the machine' in your head. In competition you will use this mental machine to guide and control your own movements which sail the boat.

As well as technical skills, imagery has a role to play in building tactical skills. You can use it to run through options, say at starts; or to build up a range of mentally rehearsed strategies to use on the last beat against a varying number of competitors in differing conditions. You can gain a lot from going yachting with a whole bag of well-rehearsed alternative tricks up your sleeve!

Used just before a race, imagery can help you to warm-up mentally, to get into the right frame of mind to attend to the right cues and focus your attention on your goals. Many performers take the time to turn inward and get themselves properly set up before competing; they claim that the five minutes they spend on mental rehearsal just before the start can be invaluable.

IMAGERY AND CONFIDENCE

Physical skill improvements are only one benefit of mental rehearsal; you can also use it to practise emotions. By rehearsing a competitive situation with appropriate accompanying emotions, you can link good, useful feelings with the situation. When you meet it in real life, the feelings are much more likely to pop up quite automatically.

This technique is also very effective if used, usually without much relaxation, as a way of summoning up useful emotions just before a race. When you are doing this you should rehearse three or four times immediately before the start: You should aim for a break of less than a minute between rehearsal and actual performance. If the break is longer than this the effect of the mental rehearsal will be greatly diminished. So you are most likely to use this technique after the five-minute gun has gone – especially if you want to improve your starts by being, say, more aggressive.

You can also link imagery and emotions to help build self-confidence. Make your rehearsal as accurate as possible by imagining the conditions, the committee boat, the other competitors, the start, the race, and your own performance in vivid detail. Most importantly, you should imagine success in achieving the performance and process goals you have set, and really appreciate how good that feels.

3 INOCULATING YOURSELF AGAINST STRESS

A particularly effective strategy is to use mental rehearsal to imagine yourself coping well under conditions of acute stress or when an unexpected disaster strikes. This is an excellent way to both increase your self-confidence and build up your resistance to stress. It has much in common with the frequent simulation exercises which airline pilots have to undertake. You should not only imagine the skill aspect, but the way you feel when you succeed. Feel good: you did it all on your own, and deserve to feel successful, confident and powerful.

You can also use mental rehearsal to recover self-confidence after making a mistake, by the mental equivalent of getting back on the horse after a fall. This technique is known as re-editing. Re-run the race up to, but not including, the mistake. Then simply imagine a successful completion (as you would in a pre-run). If you do this about five times you will have largely over-written the incident in your memory. Of course, if you have just sailed the perfect race then re-run *that* five times, and increase your memories of success!

What you must *not* do is to believe old wive's tales such as 'You learn from your mistakes'. If you re-run the mistake, you are mentally rehearsing how to do it even better, now how to avoid it! So make very sure that you go through the process above if you don't want to end up skilfully capsizing at every gybe mark . . .

OTHER USES FOR IMAGERY

Remember that the more aware you are, the better you perform. Imagery is awareness; it's not exactly the same as the awareness you get if you open your eyes, but it is sufficiently similar to be of great use. If you learn to use imagery well enough – and a lot of people can – you can try re-running successes in past races. Instead of just lying there, try 'helicoptering' so that you can get a clearer idea of what is really going on. You should try to notice what you are attending to, what you are saying to yourself and what your goals are at the moment – not just the sailing itself. See if you can relate this new knowledge to your performance.

Are you the sort of person who is perhaps a bit timid? Or too impetuous? Try imagining how you would sail if you were somebody else. This is known as 'as if' imagery, and you can use it to change the mental machine in quite subtle ways. You can even use it on the water. Just *be* that person, and sail their way. Or maybe you need to have it out with your coach, or crew.

You can rehearse interpersonal skills using the 'as if' technique, imagining you have a quite different personality.

The natural mind can often be given control by using what are called trigger words. These are words which capture the quality of the performance; you will have come across the idea before in Chapter 2. If you mentally rehearse using these trigger words, then they, like the emotions, will get ever more firmly attached to the feeling of the skill. Using them in competition helps the natural mind to recreate the skill.

PRACTISING IMAGERY

Imagery is a skill that needs to be practised, preferably daily. Ten minutes a day should do it. But before you start, try to find somewhere to relax. The reason for this is quite simple; if you have lots of incoming messages from your eyes, ears, body and conscious mind, these will probably overwhelm the fainter imagery you are trying to conjure up. Many top sailors do their mental rehearsal in bed, before falling asleep. If you can relax properly, try to stay at a relatively light level of relaxation in case you drop off. Otherwise just go floppy, breathe deeply for a minute or two, and start rehearsing.

You may find it helpful to systematise your imagery and mental rehearsal. Using the goalsetting system, you can identify areas to work on, in training and in bed. If may also help you to keep a log of what you do. This can contain comments about how you feel as mental rehearsal proceeds, so that you can see improvements as they build up.

Imagery is not hypnosis, nor is it magical. It's no use fantasising about unrealistic levels of performance in the hope that you will suddenly make a quantum leap into the superstar league. Think of imagery as a vitamin supplement; it can complement physical practice, it can be an adjunct to goalsetting, but it won't turn you into a champion overnight!

6 Concentration: the key to it all ———————

In sailing, perhaps more than any other sport, the skills of maintaining and regaining your attention focus can affect performance dramatically. This is simply because of the very long time-scales involved in sailing competition. A high-board diver needs to maintain his focus for only a few seconds, a footballer for 90 minutes. Competitive sailors may need to stay focused for anything up to 20 hours in a regatta, depending on the conditions.

In part, attention control is the skill of directing your attention to the right thoughts and cues, rather than those which will interfere with your sailing performance. That is what enables you to sail 'naturally'. It is also the skill of regaining the right focus, should your attention wander.

This chapter explains attention control, and suggests a number of ways you can improve your own. As you read it, you will see that it refers to much of what you already know about mind sailing. That is because attention control permeates much of mental training.

The problem with sailing is that you need to attend to what the fleet are doing, too. They can be all over the show, so the blinkers need to come off sometimes. This sort of attention control is quite different from the previous sort. It involves taking in information from all around you. If you have been involved in certain kinds of meditation or yoga you may have come across this very different kind of concentration.

In Part One you read about the importance of learning to sail naturally, or 'going with the flow'. In large measure this is about learning ways to keep your conscious mind under control. Unfortunately, focused attention to the workings of the conscious mind tends to occur in high-pressure situations, and the outside world and the broad perspective can all too easily get lost. And because we are attending to conscious thoughts, these can increase the pressure still further! It is useful to be aware of this, and even more useful to learn some techniques which can help overcome this limiting effect.

ATTENTION CONTROL

You may have been surprised to learn that concentrating is a skill. Actually, you learnt one sort of attention-control skill by accident in school. It is the intense, 'blinkered' sort of attention you need to read a book, work through a theoretical argument or reach a logical conclusion. A furrowed brow often shows that someone is concentrating in this way. If you get really good at this, extraneous events are largely shut out and you may not even hear people talking to you. Rally drivers call this the 'red mist', and speak of people driving straight on at a bend because they were concentrating too hard on keeping the car going fast. So this sort of attention has its drawbacks.

STAYING IN THE HERE-AND-NOW

One of the fundamental truths about competitive sailing is that it occurs in real time. Anything from another time is totally irrelevant. Many people have found that thoughts about previous failures or imminent success have caused them problems in races.

Unfortunately there is no easy answer to the problem of how to live in the present. Appropriate goalsetting, confidence management, mental relaxation strategies and self-talk techniques all have a part to play. All these techniques contain common elements, and help you to dissociate and desensitise yourself to attention-demanding, but completely irrelevant messages from your conscious mind.

1 DIFFERENT WAYS OF CONCENTRATING

Have a look at the diagram; it has two dimensions. The first is about where you focus your attention – inside your head, or outside in the real world. The second dimension is about the type of focus – broad and sweeping, or narrow and specific. Together, these dimensions describe just about all the ways you can change your attention. All of these are important, and people who are really good at concentrating can switch between them at will.

In sailing, more than any other sport, you need to be able to keep your attention moving around the four quadrants. You need broadly focused attention to assess situations and analyse them; you need narrowly focused attention to prepare for action and perform a skill. Again and again, hour after hour, day after day as the regatta unfolds you will have to change your attention style. That is why learning to control your attention is such an important skill in sailing.

```
                      BROAD FOCUS

              ANALYSE    |    ASSESS
                         |
   INTERNAL ─────────────┼───────────── EXTERNAL
                         |
              PREPARE    |    ACT

                     NARROW FOCUS
```

You can undertake concentration training programmes which claim to improve your ability to concentrate. There is no doubt that for some people, in certain sports, these programmes can be very helpful. But in our experience these programmes are too simplistic for the sport of sailing, which needs very sophisticated attention management. In any case, learning concentration skills on their own is only half the story; you need something to concentrate *on*.

The best things to focus on are the process goals which underpin your performance. This is where the goalsetting 'target' is invaluable, since it helps to identify exact-ly what you need to do in the boat to make it go fast, and what you need to think about. Ideally you should have identified a set of process goals for each leg of the race. The focus for these process goals can be wide or narrow. You may be focused on some precise quality of your sailing, such as 'floating downwind' or 'speed across the boat in tacks'. Or it may be some more general source of information outside the boat, such as what the rest of the fleet are doing, or where the windshifts are coming from.

Having process goals to focus on can be very effective as a way of keeping you in the here and now, and making sure that the

2 GOING WITH THE FLOW

If you feel that you are at one with the boat, or 'going with the flow', this means that for a short period you have managed to attend completely to process goals and their associated sensory cues, and your performance is the better for it. In other words you are sailing with your natural mind in full control, and your conscious mind has stopped generating self-talk or imagery to distract you. It's good to reach this state – all the best performers report that it happens occasionally, no matter what their sport. It's a peak experience, and we hope you get lots of those!

boat performs as it should. But that's not all. Because you are out of your conscious mind, appropriate focus can also help keep anxiety at an optimum level. So don't just go yachting and try to win; get some process goals sorted, and try to focus on them as you sail round the course.

RE-FOCUSING

It is inevitable that, at some time or other, you will lose focus. On the water this will usually mean that you are back in your conscious mind – worrying, being resentful, and all the rest of it, or you may get a version of the rally-driver's 'red mist' and be so focused on, say, boatspeed, that you fail to notice the opposition sailing past. In either case you will need to learn some strategies to help you get back to a more appropriate focus. Back on shore, after a particularly bad race, you may need to de-focus, and leave the racing behind so that you can recuperate. The strategies you may find helpful for these situations are very different.

On the water
Have you ever experienced a situation where the fleet sailed over you when you were sailing to your limit? If so, what may have happened was that you were in a narrow external focus, and the broad external focus needed for tactical decision-making

was lost. One way to avoid this happening is to get into the habit of checking on the 'fluidity' of your concentration. If it's glued-up you may miss things which are important. Just asking yourself – or your partner in the boat – to rate the fluidity of concentration on the 1-to-10 scale will often do the trick.

You may also need to shift your attention away from your conscious mind and its anxiety-producing thoughts, and back to sailing the boat. You will obviously need to be aware of what is happening; if you sit in the boat, unaware that your slow progress and rising blood-pressure are related to your thoughts, you certainly cannot expect to control the situation. It may help to do the exercise in Box 3, page 30.

In that chapter you will have encountered the technique of centering. Centering is a particularly valuable technique for refocusing, as well as controlling anxiety, simply because it takes you 'out of your head' for a moment. For example, on the mark rounding it can be used as a first move in a strategy to take attention away from negative thoughts (especially 'win' thoughts, attempts by opponents to psych you out, fear of capsize, etc.), followed by a self-instruction to focus on the next process goals.

Off the water
After a bad race, most sailors feel pretty bad. Anger, frustration, resentment and despair are all very powerful emotions, and

if you take them back on the water the next day they are not exactly guaranteed to help you perform at your best.

The feelings are real, and they need to be accepted as such. Talking them out can help, especially with a coach. Writing them down helps too, but at some point they must be discarded. That race is history, and the feelings are history, too. Remember, the black box technique? You can use a similar technique to 'lose' feelings and thoughts you no longer need. Take a walk along the beach, or out on a jetty, and throw those out-of-date feelings into the water. Watch them sink, never to return. Park them in a garage, throw them out the window, write them down and burn the paper – make up your own, personally meaningful technique.

Then start rebuilding your confidence by returning to positive thoughts about yourself, and plan what to do tomorrow. That means process goalsetting again! In this way you replace thoughts of failure with thoughts that may bring success. Then you can let it all go out of your mind until the morning.

DE-FOCUSING

If you stay fully focused while you are sailing, you also need to de-focus when you are not. Many sailors have excellent strategies for achieving this, often involving inebriating substances and the opposite sex. However, if you find yourself getting up-tight after racing and you are not the sort of person who finds it easy to join in the fun and games, you may need to actively plan some activities which enable you to recuperate.

This need not be anything very special – reading a book, playing with your computer, going to the cinema. In effect, what you are doing is giving yourself some simple, positive goals which avoid the negative goal of 'mustn't worry about tomorrow'.

Worrying about tomorrow can get really bad when you are trying to get to sleep. If you have planned some good distractions for earlier in the evening, then sleep may come quite easily. If it doesn't, don't worry. Research shows that sleep deprivation does not affect mental or physical performance, so long as you have about four hours' worth and the adrenalin flows on the day. However, if you still think 'a good night's rest' is important, try avoiding coffee or tea before going to bed. Better still, practise your relaxation skills. Or use thought stopping, followed by a self-instruction like 'Go to sleep'. That works quite well, especially if you have practised it when not racing.

The main thing is not to worry about lack of sleep. If you are trying really hard to drop off, you are wasting your time. It is much better to accept that your body wants more time awake, and take care not to use that time focusing on tomorrow's race. Get up, read a book, and make sure that you stay de-focused until sleep overtakes you.

ATTENTION IS THE KEY

Most people think of skills in physical terms – ball skills, driving skills, sailing skills, whatever. In fact, while physical skills are what people see, they depend on the skill of directing one's attention to just the right place, at the right time, and keeping it there. Unless you can do this, you will never reach your physical potential.

Mental skills also depend heavily on being able to attend to the right thoughts and stay 'on track' in your head. Unless you can do this you will never reach your mental potential.

Together, excellent physical and mental skills enable you to reach the highest levels of performance. The key to both is attention control.

7 Sailing together ───────────────

Most sailing is done in boats where two or more people are needed to perform all the tasks on board. And yet the skill involved in sailing together is an area which almost all sailors ignore. How many boats have you seen sailing back to the slipway with tense, tight-lipped crews? Perhaps you sail with your spouse or partner; the interpersonal dynamics involved here often lead to fiery interchanges on board – and later! Or you may have tried several times to find a helm or crew you can get on with, and begun to despair of ever getting it together.

It is very common for each person on a boat to be completely fed up with the other. Sadly, the reasons for this seldom get discussed, let along addressed, and promising partnerships often break up acrimoniously. This happens at all levels in sailing, and yet a basic rule for efficient and effective competitive sailing is that discord in the boat should be avoided like the plague. The reason for this is quite simple. Boatspeed depends on both the helm and the crew's attention staying focused on the task of sailing. If you are falling out with each other, bottling up fury or fantasising about how it might have been – the boat goes slower.

This chapter will help you understand a number of things which can happen when people are trying to cooperate. Usually, these lead to conflict. It also describes some techniques to make conflict less likely, or more manageable if it does occur.

FRUSTRATION AND ANGER

A common experience for many people who sail together is that the level of tension on the boat reaches boiling point. The helm and the crew get frustrated and angry, and a shouting match develops. So what is going on – and more importantly, how can you control the situation?

When you are highly motivated to do something and your success is threatened, frustration is the natural and inevitable result. Frustration is a primitive mechanism rather like an overdrive, which makes you try harder. A continuing block can produce anger: a sort of emergency boost which can sometimes mobilise the energy you need to blast through the block. Unfortunately it is all too easy to see the person you sail with as the block, and all that frustration and anger gets directed at him.

The thing to remember is that frustration and anger are normal, but primitive emotional and physical responses which, like anxiety, have the simple purpose of raising your activation levels. They are not remotely rational reactions and, indeed, may actually prevent you being rational at the time. It is easy to forget that, in reality, your partner in the boat is the one person who can help you be successful. Apart from staying rational in competitive conditions, your mental and physical arousal levels should be at their optimum. Further increases may actually *decrease* your effectiveness, or lead to a complete blow-out. It is therefore important to have ways of reducing your arousal.

It is all too easy to let the tension build until it is catastrophically high, by which time it may be too late to remedy the situation. Nobody actually likes the feeling of being tense, but it is possible you may not notice the tenseness in the hurly-burly of sailing at the limit. The simple way to ensure that you become more aware of tension is to agree to monitor tension levels in the boat. If it gets too high, someone – anyone – should say 'Tension in the boat is about 7 or 8'. In the 1992 Olympic campaign, several boats using this tactic found that it enabled them to contain potentially explosive situations before they became unmanageable.

However, you may need to go further. You have already read about two useful techniques – centering and mastery statements – which may help you to regain control. Centering can take your attention away from the immediate problem for just long enough to let activation levels drop to a less critical level. On the other hand, it may be that appropriate self-talk is right for you in certain circumstances. You can use this to control yourself (for example 'I stay calm', 'I understand what is happening and I refuse to be upset'). You must make up your own phrases – it's your self-talk.

RESENTMENT

One thing that can happen over a period of time is that one – or both – of you builds up a degree of resentment towards the other. Unlike normal and natural responses of fear and anger to external stressors, such as oncoming ferries, or the crew falling off the wire on the last beat, resentment is an entirely mental phenomenon. Basically, resentment is a sort of fantasy anger, aroused by imagery of a negative kind. In theory, the cure is simple – you need to replace the negative fantasies with more positive images of your partner.

Those negative images are almost certainly of some past event, such as a mistake in a previous race, which you are recalling and using to generate this pseudo-anger. There is nothing you can do to change history, but being resentful of the past is not helping you to sail well together in the present. It is, however, possible to combat resentment by looking afresh at history, using your deep relaxation and visualising skills.

Changing your negative fantasies for more positive ones is a three-stage process.
1 Visualise *positive* things happening to your partner, things such as being happy, being successful, sailing perfectly. This will help you see him in a different light.
2 Revisualise the events that rankle with you, but this time see them from the point of view of your partner. Feel what he felt, as he made the mistake. Did he mean to? Was he pleased? This will help you to see things from a different perspective.
3 Finally, again from his point of view, see how he saw *your* part in the scenario and feel how he felt about your reactions to him. Did you help him learn from it? Or did you hinder the development of your relationship? How could you be more effective?

This reprogramming of the way you think about your partner and your relationship to him may enable you to start thinking and feeling more positively about the person you rely on most of all.

CONFIDENCE AND CONFLICT

The sum total of the feelings that you each have about your self-worth and your ability to perform well are the 'psychological batteries' which enable you to use your skills and experience to their maximum. They need to stay as fully charged as possible, since confidence is probably the key factor which wins races when boats are closely matched on speed and skills. It is very important to be aware that the *combined* confidence of both crew-members is involved – it is no use, for example, the crew feeling superconfident if the helm is despondent about everything – including himself.

You might think that you should therefore be very protective of your confidence. This is true, but it is critically important to do this in the right way. The problem is that sometimes you may try to protect yourself at the expense of the other person's self-confidence. For example, you might cope with your own failure by making it appear to be someone else's 'fault'. This is known as scapegoating, or playing the 'I'm OK, you're not OK' game.

Playing the 'You're not OK' game is an immature way of dealing with threats to your own self-confidence. It is much used by children ('I'm better than you, so there'). In reality, many adults never learn to change their immature strategies. Successful relationships of all types are built on behaving in adult ways, and there is no doubt that learning to think and behave in a more adult way is difficult. Newspaper stories about multiple marriages are testimony to this.

If you suspect that immature game-playing is going on in your boat, you may consider it worth developing personal and inter-personal skills to control the situation. Otherwise it will almost certainly escalate, and a promising combination of helm and crew may come to blows.

The first step is to ask yourself if destructive games are being played in your boat. Do not underestimate how difficult this can be. You may be so used to being a player in these games that they seem like second nature, but they needn't be.

Then try to determine who is most heavily involved. It is in the nature of these things that both of you may be, although there is almost always one person who starts it. If he can change, the other person may well follow suit.

Clues which will help you decide whether you are being protective of yourself at your partner's expense may be found in the way you speak to him. If you are using a scolding tone of voice; words like 'stupid', 'care-less' or 'brainless'; phrases like, 'how many time have I told you', and especially 'you should', or 'you ought'; if you are using physical cues such as horrified glances, tongue-clicking, eye-rolling, pursing your lips or sighing, then you are definitely NOT doing anybody any good, except yourself in the short term.

You will know if you are on the receiving end of someone's self-protective anger if your lip is quivering, your shoulders shrug, you squirm, giggle, stick your tongue out or have a temper-tantrum — all the sort of things toddlers do when they are told off. Your partner is not treating you as an adult, so you feel like a three-year-old and behave accordingly. If any of these things are happening to you when things are not going well, you are being scapegoated.

If you recognise any of this you have problems, but do not despair. You can develop ways to manage the situation. There are two approaches which can help you: The first is to try to contain it, the second is to try to prevent it occurring.

Coping with conflict

Containment strategies operate at the individual level. If you feel frustrated and angry with your partner, you can use self-talk to remind you how to manage your anger ('When I feel angry, I centre for five breaths, and then get back to sailing the boat'). If your activation levels are not too high, you can remind yourself to use the extra energy creatively ('I feel angry, so I focus it on the opposition'). These tactics may help you avoid starting an unpleasant scene.

The person who is on the receiving end of another's fury can protect his own self-confidence by using 'Rights' to erect a barrier between himself and his actions. Suppose the crew slips up badly and the helm lashes out 'You stupid idiot, you ought to know better by now!' If the crew uses self-talk such as 'I know you are frustrated, but I have a right to make mistakes', he can use that to minimise the impact of the understandable outburst. This is a passive response, and the crew must learn to refrain from the old ways of countering such a threat by snapping back 'Sucks to you, too!' A more sophisticated method is to learn how to accept such criticism – not to be threatened by it, but to recognise it for what it may be: a destructive confidence-management strategy. Of course, you also need to react sensibly to useful criticism. Underlying this technique is the very important concept of openness; games such as 'You're not OK' prevent openness because they are designed to obscure the fact that the perpetrator of the verbal violence is actually under threat himself. Accept this by saying 'Sorry, you must be really upset by my mistake' and the value of the game becomes vanishingly small. And, more importantly, reality breaks out.

Preventing conflict

The most powerful strategy of all is to use techniques which weld the crew and helm together into a cohesive whole, so that the potential for conflict is minimised. It will help you to understand how these work if you know a little about how small groups of people change as they form into teams. These changes have been observed many times, and described in several ways. Box 1 (overleaf) explains one of the more understandable models of the process.

Luckily, the ways in which you can develop the right sort of relationships in the boat are now fairly well understood. The three keys to forming and maintaining a cohesive crew are good communication, clear roles and effective goalsetting. But the whole thing pivots on the trust created by shared commitment.

IMPROVING COMMUNICATION

It is quite common to find that many sailors, even at the highest level, have major communication difficulties; they may never sit down and talk about anything other than race tactics, boat tuning or travel arrangements. Unless communication is wide-ranging, open and honest, suspicion and paranoia are the almost inevitable result. Nobody is a mind reader; on the contrary, most people easily misinterpret the actions of others. This can be a recipe for disaster.

If you are going to sail together you will need to have business meetings, where the nuts and bolts of your campaign are clearly worked out and understood. But it is also important to remember that you are not machines, and that you should spend some time finding out about each other at various human levels, too.

Can you get along together socially? You are going to have to if, like many people, you share a room or the back of a van while you are out on the circuit. That is when you find out the little things that may grow from niggles to the straw that breaks the camel's

1 TEAM DEVELOPMENT ON A BIG RACING YACHT

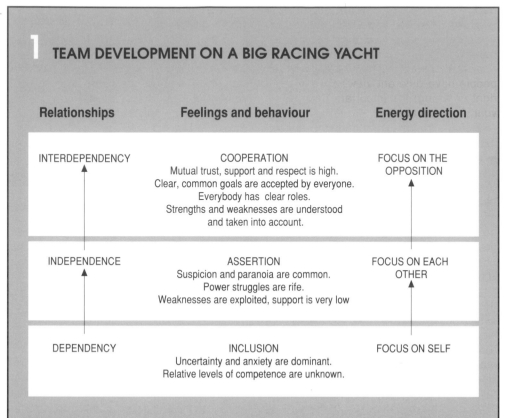

Relationships	Feelings and behaviour	Energy direction
INTERDEPENDENCY	COOPERATION Mutual trust, support and respect is high. Clear, common goals are accepted by everyone. Everybody has clear roles. Strengths and weaknesses are understood and taken into account.	FOCUS ON THE OPPOSITION
INDEPENDENCE	ASSERTION Suspicion and paranoia are common. Power struggles are rife. Weaknesses are exploited, support is very low	FOCUS ON EACH OTHER
DEPENDENCY	INCLUSION Uncertainty and anxiety are dominant. Relative levels of competence are unknown.	FOCUS ON SELF

The first stage is called *inclusion.* This is the time during which the predominant question in the crew member's mind is 'Do I belong here?' or 'Do I feel included?' Crew members will be a little withdrawn and tentative. This is in contrast to the second stage, known as the *assertion* stage, in which many members' behaviour will be distinctly assertive. It is the stage in which the pecking order is established. Each member is looking to see where he fits, but is also flexing his muscles to establish his power. Inevitably there is a certain amount of interpersonal competitiveness within the crew which wastes much of the energy and attention which would otherwise be spent on getting the job done.

This is where most crews are, most of the time. Only rarely do crews achieve the third stage which is the *cooperation* stage. If they do reach it, the crew members voluntarily set aside their individual agendas to cooperate in achieving a common goal. The weaker members are supported when they fail, (rather than rubbished, which is what happens in the assertion stage). Trust between members is very high and a genuine affection between them may develop. The focused attention of such a crew towards a clearly specified objective, such as a race, a championship or even the America's Cup, is fairly unbeatable.

The shift from one stage of the next is not sudden or clearly defined and, unfortunately, the third stage is a relatively rare occurrence unless the group has been willing to use specific techniques to achieve it.

back. It is important to develop good, open communication from the start so that differences can be aired, and behaviours agreed between you. For example, are you going to drink in the evenings at regattas? Different people have different viewpoints. None is right or wrong; the important thing is that your views are aired.

Being irritated by someone's personal habits is going to get in the way, both socially and when you're sailing. You can either say something (which gives him the option of changing the habit) or learn to accept his habits for the sake of getting the best crewman going. That choice is yours. Either way, be clear about your choice; don't simply say nothing and fume. But if you are going to discuss the matter, first put yourself in his shoes. In what way would you like to be told about your pet mannerism? That's probably the best way to tell him. Before you start campaigning in earnest, go sailing with the objective of finding all the differences you have in approach. Air the problems, and make agreements that you can live with. Once an agreement is made, keep to it.

This is vital. If you don't really mean to stick to your agreement, if you don't recognise its value, if you're only saying yes because we say you should, forget it.

If you want to take communication to its logical conclusion, you may want to consider a technique used by many Olympic crews. The precise form of words that you use to communicate with each other in the boat can be the source of much conflict in the stress of competition. People vary a lot in their sensitivity to words, but everyone has a 'crumple button' which reacts to very specific taunts. Equally, everyone needs a bit of support, particularly from their partner on the boat. So if you need the helm to say 'Good luck today' as you sail out to the course, or if the crew's frustrated 'You're not trying' is like a match to your blue touchpaper, discuss it. If you can agree to use words and phrases which both find acceptable, that can be very effective in keeping the peace on board.

Agreeing roles

Getting roles sorted out is not just about who sits where in the boat. It is also about knowing what the other wants from you — calling out opposition positions, windshifts or compass headings, perhaps; keeping up a continuous stream of positive comments about this performance; being the joker who keeps the atmosphere sweet. Whatever it may be, being clear and confident about one's role in the boat is very important.

Sometimes you find that somebody is good at one thing, but wants to do another.If the crew has a desire to do the tuning, let him do it! 'OK, while I'm on boatspeed you tweak the rig. We'll try that in the next practice session and for the first race, and monitor it carefully. But let's agree now to change the arrangement after the race if need be.' Either he'll become good at tuning, or he'll find he hasn't a clue and will stop the stream of 'helpful' suggestions. Whatever happens the boat will gain.

It can be just as important to sort out the off-the-water roles. Who gets the cover off the boat? Who decides what time you reach the boat park? Who does the cooking? Can you each spend equal amounts of time on training, working on the boat and racing? And whose job is it to raise sponsorship, book travel arrangements and so on? An equitable arrangement is normally easy to find. For example, one person may really enjoy making the boat look immaculate; another may be a born organiser. Experience shows that it is vital to get these mundane things sorted, otherwise guilt and resentment can overwhelm the best-matched crew in the world.

Setting your goals

It goes without saying that you and the other member of the crew should look very closely at your goals, such as winning a championship.

You need to define your goal, then look at your respective levels of commitment to it. You should be willing to talk for hours about this. If you find you have different

2 A CONTRACT

This is an example of a real contract made between a helm and crew of an Olympic class dinghy in 1990. Jack was the helm, and John was the crew. Can you appreciate what the difficulty was on this boat? Do you think they succeeded in remedying it?

1 Both agree that they will commit themselves as fully as they possibly can to their joint goals. These are:
a) to compete in the World Championships in 1990; and
b) to compete in the Olympic Games in 1992.
Both hope to win at these competitions, but recognise that winning is a goal which is outside their control, and therefore should not form part of a goalsetting programme.

2 Each recognises that they are equal and interdependent members of a two-man team. Without the other person's skills in the boat, their goals cannot be achieved. They each respect, and acknowledge, these skills in the other.

3 Together they agree to improve communication between them. This means, specifically:
a) After regattas, they will review their performance. Positive aspects will be discussed first; mistakes will be regarded as learning opportunities in discussion; and all positive and constructive comments will be reviewed at the end of the discussion;
b) They will keep in touch at least twice a week when not sailing.

4 John agrees to ensure that, in the boat, Jack is aware of his high level of commitment to his tasks as a crew. If he is asked for information which he does not immediately know, he will say 'Hold on' assertively, so that Jack is aware that he is responding positively to his request.

5 John's ability to control his arousal under stress is a positive advantage in the boat. Jack agrees to perceive it as such, and not as evidence of lack of commitment. This will involve some mental reprogramming, which he agrees to do.

6 Both agree that it is unacceptable, and counter-productive, for Jack to direct his aggression at John should either make a mistake. If a mistake, by either of them, should occur, they agree to say 'Forget it'. This is understood to be a cue to:
a) refocus attention on the present task of sailing the boat; and
b) return to this problem, if necessary, after the race, in order to learn from it.
In addition, John agrees to learn to use 'rights' to give himself a degree of protection should a breach of this occur.

7 Jack now understands that John responds well to positive comments, and will use them frequently. This will build their joint esteem, on which their success ultimately depends. John undertakes to use self-affirmation statements to build his resistance to negative comments by others.

objectives don't gloss over the fact. Be honest with each other about your doubts, and bear in mind that it's impossible to persuade someone to change an objective. Simply talking about your differences may well lead to alignment, or at least to someone suspending his objective till later.

Often you will not have seen the person clearly; you may have heard that he is difficult to sail with, projected that image onto him, then disliked the way he behaves. He may in fact be a joy to sail with provided he can find a helmsman as committed as he is himself, with whom he can share a common goal.

Making a commitment

It is fine to share an understanding of each other's roles and goals, and particularly the rules governing behaviour, but it is equally important to make a commitment to abide by these rules.This shared commitment can lead to trust in each other.Trust can take a long time to develop, and it may never happen spontaneously, but it can certainly be encouraged if you make the rules explicit and make a joint agreement to abide by them.

Such joint agreements are called contracts, because they clearly set out how two parties are to relate to each other in the future. Many team sports use them, and a dinghy crew is a small, two-person team. Just like business contracts, they need to be negotiated until both sides feel they have a fair deal; they need to be written down; and, ideally, they need to be formally signed! It is even better if they are then made public, like marriage vows. Coaches and spouses are probably a big enough public, but you might want to consider the club noticeboard if you need the maximum effect.

Many Olympic boats used contracts to help them stay focused and cooperating under the intensely competitive pressures of the 1992 campaign. A typical Olympic dinghy crew contract is shown in Box 2 to help to focus your ideas a bit. It states the joint performance goals, both long-term and short-term, and it specifies some of the process goals which each will try to reach to make achieving those performance goals more likely. Some of these are about how they should think and behave; some are about how they should speak to each other. The point of these contracts is that they enhance what psychologists call task cohesion – the degree to which each member of the crew is committed to their joint aims and objectives. A contract simply makes the different types of goal as clear as possible, so that individual commitment is raised. Research shows quite clearly that when task cohesion is high, performance is also high.

However, do bear in mind that making a contract is not a cure-all. Ultimately, if you cannot stand each other, no contract in the world is going to keep you together! Growing to like your partner in the boat is evidence for the development of a very different sort of cohesion, called social cohesion. Research also shows that when social cohesion is high, performance can be low; you are probably spending a lot of time in the bar together! If that's the kind of sailing you go in for, that's fine too; not everybody wants to compete internationally.

Task cohesion does not require social cohesion. In many high-performing boats there is little love lost between the helm and crew. They simply get on with the job. You may not want to sail with quite such single-minded determination; nevertheless, if you can agree a contract, you may find it a very helpful exercise. Deciding on the best form of words and discussing the topics fully is in itself a most valuable exercise in communication; it helps you get your roles clear and set effective joint goals. Good luck!

PART THREE

BODY SAILING

This section of the book is aimed at the club-level sailor with international aspirations. It provides some informative ideas and guidance on the most efficient method of improving fitness for those of you trying to achieve that extra one per cent. It does not and cannot provide a comprehensive guide to every form of exercise or machine ever designed.

Instead, it acts as a guide to the general exercise required for your particular branch of the sport, and provides a sound base for individual development in a logical and progressive manner. It is up to you to select the techniques appropriate to your own needs. Obviously anyone who is extremely overweight, over 35 years of age and beginning an exercise programme, pregnant or suffering from a medical disorder should seek advice from a doctor. Sailors under 16 years of age should not use weights (other than body weight) for training.

In this section we have chosen to categorise sailors in four very broad categories: Windsurfer, hiker, trapezer and keelboat crew, but in some cases we have gone into detail. For example, the requirements of a Finn/Laser/Europe hiker are similar but not identical to the requirement of a 470/Fireball helm, so the differences have been discussed.

Fitting it all in

It is a common misconception that it takes a long time to make significant improvements to fitness; hence the common excuse that 'I won't be able to find the time!'. Nonsense! Pleading inadequate time to undertake more commitments simply indicates poor time management and slack goalsetting – both of which should be improved by your psychological training. By setting effective goals you can easily create time for a fitness programme.

In any case, modern techniques have vastly reduced the time needed for physical training. And because you can go sailing to get *fit* for sailing – as long as the conditions are appropriate – you may have to make only minimal changes to your current lifestyle. Something in the order of three of four hours per week should do it.

So, no excuses – get fit!

1 Fitness and sailing

Many people sail simply because they enjoy it, and they get fit enough to sail at the level they want by racing each weekend. But if you are trying to get to the top, the long hours you spend on the water honing your skills will almost certainly need to be supplemented by additional physical training. For although full-time sailing can be an excellent way to improve your physical fitness, you cannot rely exclusively on this method of physical conditioning. Good, strenuous conditions cannot always be guaranteed, and even if conditions are ideal the time taken to get to the club, rig the boat and so on means that the actual time on the water is limited.

Additional on-land training provides variety, can be made interesting and enjoyable and helps you avoid spending too much time on the water for the wrong reasons and getting stale. Most of all, exercises to overload the body and make it adapt can be developed in a very much more controlled and efficient way than you could ever hope for in your boat.

How fit do you need to be?
Fitness is a relative term, and both the type and level of fitness required by sailors may differ depending on the boat or board and whether you are the helm or crew. It is also important to remember that the level at which you are sailing has implications for your fitness requirements. You need to strike a balance between fitness and all the other aspects of your sailing.

WHAT IS FITNESS?

Fitness is made up of several components. Essentially, these are stamina, strength, flexibility, speed and skill. For a given sport, the mix and relative importance of the components will be very different. Think about

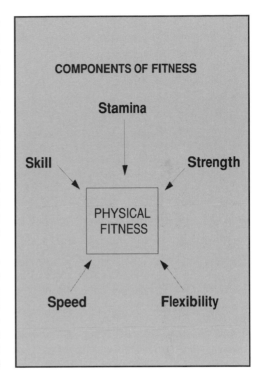

weightlifting, sprinting and sailing: what do you think the mix would be in each of these?

Stamina
Stamina is the ability to keep going, otherwise known as endurance. It has two main elements:

Aerobic endurance refers to the ability of the body to keep going for an extended period. This is a fundamental requirement for any sport and can be developed to a reasonable level over about 12 weeks by activities which emphasise duration rather than intense effort, such as running, cycling, swimming, circuit training and aerobics. It can also be improved by sailing, in the right conditions. Unfortunately this takes too much time; there are more efficient ways to develop aerobic endurance on land.

Muscular endurance refers to the capacity of a muscle or a group of muscles to work continuously against loads. One way it can be developed is by circuit training, either with or without weights. Once muscles have adapted to this form of work they can operate for longer before fatigue sets in. This type of fitness is vital in sailing. For example, holding the mainsheet in a force 5 is a strenuous activity, and the helm may need to keep it up for quite a long time.

Strength

Strength is about exerting force through muscular effort. It can be developed by progress in resistance training, better known as weight training. Strength can be acquired generally or targeted at a specific body part, such as weak arms.

Sailing demands a certain amount of strength for many tasks. Hauling the main halyard of a keelboat, for example, demands considerable muscular effort.

Flexibility

This is the ability to move your joints freely over a wide range without risking injury. It is achieved by stretching, which should be a part of *every* training session both on land and on the water. It is all too easy to neglect this. Sailors often operate in a very hostile sporting environment – cold, wet and often miserable – and sit doing virtually nothing while waiting for the start gun. They then go straight into the race without warming up by stretching. No other sport has been so slow to incorporate stretching as part of an injury prevention programme.

Speed

In a technical sense this implies explosive actions, but in sailing these are not often required. Keelboat crews are the most in need of speed training, to prepare them for winch grinding or hoisting spinnakers.

Skill

Fitness can prepare your body to act efficiently, but you still need to be able to carry out certain actions effectively. For this you need skill. Sailing is a high-skill sport requiring balance and coordination. These can be developed through specific skill training.

As you can see, fitness is quite a complex subject. But if you get your fitness levels right for the type of sailing you do and the class of boat you sail, your ability to compete effectively will almost certainly improve.

WHY GET FIT?

There are several reasons why improving your fitness levels will improve your sailing, but here we will concentrate on two of the most important ones – reducing your susceptibility to fatigue and getting your weight right for your own boat.

Most sailors are all too painfully aware that, at the beginning of the season, it hurts to hike for ten minutes, yet after a couple of months it only hurts after 25 minutes. The reason is that you have got fitter, and you are less prone to fatigue.

What happens when it hurts? You start thinking about the pain, instead of sailing the boat. Your skill levels deteriorate quite rapidly – wandering concentration on the last beat or capsizing are often symptoms of fatigue. At the start of the race you probably work flat out, keeping the boat level, constantly tuning, hiking on the gusts and waves. But as the race progresses you pay less attention to some of these details. Why? If they were important at the beginning, they are important at the end! Fatigue is the reason.

Training can and does delay the onset of fatigue, and being able to out-think or out-tack a fatigued opponent on the final beat could give *you* that extra one per cent. Similarly, your recovery time between one race and the next can be reduced by increased levels of fitness. At international level sailors often compete in two or three consecutive regattas, so the need for swift recovery becomes vital.

Most types of sailing craft require their helms and crews to fit into an optimum weight category. Too little weight will slow you down in medium and heavy air; too much weight will cause problems in light winds. At Olympic level, and at the top of the Laser class, the optimum weight bands are so narrow that weight is a vital factor in performance. If you are looking to gain or lose weight, training can be of help.

You may be considering temporarily increasing your weight by wearing a weight jacket. Some classes still allow weight to be carried by the helm and crew, but without proper physical training to prepare the body for these loads, the risk of injury is greatly increased. If you intend to wear weights to the limit of the class rules then you should add it in small amounts – both in race training and competition – to acclimatise your body to the unnatural strain. If you suffer from back injury, are not in current regular training or are still growing YOU SHOULD NOT WEAR A WEIGHT JACKET.

IS TRAINING FOR YOU?

Now that you appreciate why physical fitness is an important factor in competitive sailing performance, you may be feeling that getting fitter is a good thing. Before you embark on a training programme, however, you need to think about five factors which determine the type of training you do and the likelihood of success. These are your:
- Age.
- Current health status.
- Individual circumstances.
- Commitment level.
- Organisational skill.

Let's look at each in turn.

Your age
Both younger and older sailors should be careful when undertaking physical training programmes. If you are in the younger age bracket and you are still growing, your body is very adaptable and fitness training can be especially effective, but you must be cautious about undertaking weight training until you are fully mature. Before puberty you should stick to multi-gym exercises which you can handle comfortably. That said, everyone matures at a different rate and you may be able to use weights at any time from 14 years of age. If in doubt, ask an expert.

For the older sailor, exercise can reduce obesity and control your weight. By improving the efficiency of your heart, you will also find you can pull the boat up the slip without wiping yourself out! But don't forget that, as you get older, adaptations take place more slowly and maximum capacities are reduced. It also goes without saying that there is an increased risk of heart failure if the body is stressed too much too soon. So, if you are in any doubt at all about your suitability for training, see your doctor.

Your current health status
Aspiring international sailors need to enjoy a certain level of medical health to withstand the rigours of the circuit. More importantly, if you are to train seriously you ought to check that you have no health problems which might get in the way. The list of questions in Box 1 overleaf will help you to decide whether you need to seek medical advice regarding your ability to train.

Individual circumstances
The success of a training programme depends heavily on the amount of time you have available. Fitting in a training schedule will be easy for a full-time sailor, not too hard for a student with a flexible timetable but difficult for an individual with a full-time job. You may have to seriously consider time-management! Which brings us to...

Commitment level
Whether you include an adequate fitness schedule into your programme depends to a great extent on your level of commitment. The maxim 'you can always find time for the things you really want to do' applies here. Time management without commitment is a

waste of time. Check out Box 2 to see whether you have that commitment.

Organisational skill

Effective use of your time is one skill you will need to master. We all know people who appear to be better organised than we are. It is not a problem peculiar to sailors, and the techniques of time management can be learned by most people. That is why time-management systems are so popular! So our advice is to get one!

Planning a fitness programme

This is a very individual matter. We could suggest a day-by-day workout, which you might follow slavishly – for a while. The programme you *will* follow has to be yours, since if you build it around your own circumstances, personal interests and current

1 SHOULD YOU SHOULD SEEK MEDICAL ADVICE?

Underline YES or NO in response to each question.

Do you suffer from high blood pressure?	YES	NO
Have you ever suffered from pains in the chest?	YES	NO
Do you suffer from severe breathlessness when not exercising?	YES	NO
Have you suffered from any serious illness in the last three years?	YES	NO
Have you suffered from any serious injury in the last three years?	YES	NO
Do you suffer periods of faintness, unconsciousness or dizziness?	YES	NO
Have you ever been diagnosed as having diabetes?	YES	NO
Have you ever been diagnosed as being epileptic?	YES	NO
Are you taking any medication at the present time?	YES	NO
Do you suffer from migraine attacks?	YES	NO
Do you suffer from asthma attacks?	YES	NO
Do you suffer from stomach pains or other abdominal complaints?	YES	NO
Do you have a cold, flu or any minor infection at the moment?	YES	NO
Do you have a sore throat at present?	YES	NO
Are you under any major stress?	YES	NO
Are you over 35 years of age?	YES	NO
Are you pregnant?	YES	NO

If you answered yes to one or more of these questions, or know of other factors which may affect your health, then you must consult your doctor before undertaking a fitness training programme.

2 HOW COMMITTED ARE YOU TO GETTING FIT?

Without commitment it is difficult to sustain a training regime. The following questions will improve your awareness of what is involved in getting and staying fit.

Are you prepared to exercise at least four times a week? (Including sailing if conditions are appropriate.)	YES	NO
Are you prepared to give up at least three hours a week, plus your sailing time?	YES	NO
Are you prepared to train alone?	YES	NO
If a partner or friend stopped training, would you continue?	YES	NO
Do you plan to be training in a year's time?	YES	NO
Do you plan to be training in five years' time?	YES	NO
Are you prepared to modify your work and sleeping habits?	YES	NO
Are you prepared to adjust your whole lifestyle if necessary to include areas such as diet and drinking?	YES	NO
Are you prepared to cut out one or two things you currently enjoy enormously?	YES	NO

Obviously positive answers to all these questions would be ideal, but even if you have doubts, or respond with outright negatives, at least you now have some idea of what will be required.

health status, you are much more likely to stick to it. That is why we have chosen to give you a basic understanding of the principles of physical training. You can use this knowledge to take a long-term approach to your fitness; the end result should be a fitter and healthier sailor but, just as with mental fitness, your physical fitness is *your* responsibility.

It takes about three months to get fit but only three weeks to lose it again. That is why fitness training needs to be a long-term activity. Short bursts of enthusiasm may also lead to injury and subsequent loss of motivation. So whatever your current level of fitness, make sure that you follow the golden rule: take *steady, regular* exercise with *gradual progression*.

How much, how long, what type?

The guidelines shown here apply to everybody, but analysis of your own requirements will enable you to modify and adapt these programmes to suit yourself.

There are four basic kinds of fitness training: base work, development work, specific work and maintained work. Each is concerned with different aspects of fitness and may be appropriate at different stages of your sailing year. For each we have suggested times for which you need to train and the sort of benefits you can expect.

Base work

This is where the fundamental adaptation of the body takes place. All sailors need to start with this.

BASE WORK

No of weeks: minimum 4, ideally 8-12

Type of training	Sessions per week	Length of session
Flexibility	At least 4	10-15 minutes
Aerobic	Between 2 and 4	15-45, depending on current fitness

Development work

This is where the training becomes slightly more specific to the sailor and his needs. Muscular endurance work is the main feature of this period, although you should continue with flexibility and aerobic work. Overall there should be an increase in the time spent training.

Specific work

You should carry out this work prior to resuming full weekend sailing. Simulator work is important by this stage and you should have developed a sound base for any strength training you may need. You should maintain your flexibility work, but you may have to reduce aerobic work – although

DEVELOPMENT WORK

No of weeks: minimum 4, ideally 8-10

Type of training	Sessions per week	Length of session
Muscular endurance (circuits/weights)	2-3	30-60 minutes
Aerobic	2-3	30 minutes
Flexibility	4	10-15 minutes

SPECIFIC WORK

No of weeks: minimum 4, ideally 6-10

Type of training	Sessions per week	Length of session
Flexibility	4	0-15
Muscular endurance	0-2	45
Strength	0-2	45-60
Simulator	2	15-20
Aerobic	2-3	20

not for more than two weeks at a time. The aerobic work could be combined with the simulator training. You can read more about specific training in Box 3 on the next page.

Maintenance work

You should undertake this when the main part of the racing season is underway. Sailing itself becomes an important part of the programme, although light winds may make additional work necessary. The aim here is to keep the body in good shape. You may wish to continue training: the psychological benefits can be very motivating, even if the physical effects are less important.

Training during regattas is quite a problem for international-level sailors. Obviously the priority is the racing, and often the days on the water are too long to permit training afterwards. High initial levels of fitness can help overcome this problem, as can designing a programme to maintain your levels of fitness that you can realistically carry out during periods away.

A TYPICAL WORKOUT

Every session, whether it be aerobics, circuit training, simulator or weights, should follow a three-phase pattern in which the main workout is sandwiched between a warm-up and a warm-down. Many people ignore these, but they are very important . You can read why in the next chapter.

Phase 1 – Warm-up

Aim to *raise the pulse rate* gently by walking or jogging, skipping, swimming or cycling. *Loosen up* joints such as the elbows, ankles, wrists, shoulders and back. *Stretch* to increase flexibility, particularly in those areas to be used in the workout. *Raise the pulse rate again,* since it may have dropped during stretching

Phase 2 – The main workout

This can be either aerobic or circuit training, focusing on muscular endurance or strength training using weights. You may use equipment or a simulator or both.

Phase 3 – Warm-down

Gradually *lower the pulse rate* by gentle exercise as in Phase 1, and stretch to relax your muscles and cleanse them of waste products.

REST AND RECOVERY

It is all too easy to overlook rest in training, but since this is the time when the body actually adapts it is a vital factor in acquiring

MAINTENANCE WORK

No of weeks: as required by racing season

Type of training	Sessions per week	Length of session
Muscular endurance (circuits/weights)	as required	as required
Aerobic	2-4	20-45 minutes
Flexibility	4	15-30 minutes

3 GENERAL AND SPECIFIC TRAINING

The more closely a training exercise replicates the actual actions you carry out in a boat, the greater the improvement in that action. If you are a singlehander, for example, you should train your hiking muscles and rope-pulling muscles in the same manner as when racing.

Before you start training so specifically, however, it is important to develop your general body fitness and to maintain this while working at more specific training. After all, there are many instances when sailing requires general fitness – righting a capsized boat, for example, can be extremely strenuous, yet good hiking muscles may be of little use! Accordingly most of the programmes we have outlined in this book incorporate both general and specific elements.

It is also important to keep a balance between different muscle groups on either side of a joint or series of joints. When you are training the stomach muscles, for example, you should also work on your back muscles. The sailing spectrum below illustrates the rough requirements for each broad group of sailors.

CONTINUOUS ←————————————————→ PERIODS OF
HIGH ACTIVITY   RELATIVE INACTIVITY

	Windsurfers	Hikers	Trapezers	Keel crews
Important areas to work on	grip	legs	legs	arm/shoulders
	forearms	stomach	neck	
	back	back	back	
	legs	arms	arms	
General training req'ments	flexibility	flexibility	flexibility	flexibility
	aerobic	aerobic	aerobic	some aerobic
	muscular endurance	muscular endurance	muscular endurance	some muscular endurance
	some strength	some strength	some strength	some strength

Obviously this is a simplification; the requirements of a Soling keelboat middleman or foredeck crew, for example, would be quite different to those of a One-Ton trimmer. Nevertheless it is a useful guide to general and specific training for a range of activities within the sport.

fitness. It is particularly important to get both the amount and timing of your rest correct. Following exercise, fitness levels first dip, then increase, then return to the original point as the muscles recover. So a long rest doesn't help; you need to start training again when your body is at the peak of overcompensation from the last session. If, on the other hand, you start training again too soon after exercise, the muscles are stressed before they have recovered. This is the classic over-training syndrome, with more training leading to decreased fitness.

You need to set the right pace for your training by building in the correct amount of rest at the right time. You should ensure that there is at least one day a week when you do not train, and a period each year when you give your body a holiday – which means no racing or training, except for weight maintenance.

TAKING CARE OF YOURSELF

Fitness training is supposed to make you feel better and perform better, but exercise is potentially dangerous, because you can cause yourself injury by overdoing it or by having an accident.

Make sure you use the approved clothing, footwear and equipment for the activity you are undertaking, such as good running shoes, reflective bands on your clothing, good lights on your bike and a stable platform for weights.

Check that your exercise environment is suitable:
● Is there plenty of fresh air?
● Is it warm enough?
● Is it too warm?
● Is the ground or floor appropriate? Beware of impact injuries when training on hard ground.

But don't forget the old adage – no pain, no gain. If your training is to have any effect it *is* going to be uncomfortable, but you need to know the difference between the discomfort associated with serious effort and the pain of injury. It is especially important to distinguish between the different sensations both during and after exercise:

Pain in a joint, muscle, tendon or ligament around the ankle, knee or elbow is bad news – SEEK MEDICAL ADVICE.

Soreness in the muscle itself, usually one or two days after exercise, is fairly bad news. This is a symptom of 'overdoing' it. A little gentle stretching may help, but you should wait until the soreness has disappeared before asking the muscle to do more work.

Discomfort within a working muscle may be simply a result of having made a serious effort which has led to the build up of fatigue products. This is OK.

You should avoid any exercise which is liable to cause an injury or aggravate an existing problem, and find a substitute. The most common injuries in sailing are to the back and knees. If you have an injury to these, or any other parts of your body, you SHOULD NOT TRAIN until you have received medical advice.

Proper strengthening and flexibility programmes can reduce the risk of injury. If you have a history of back problems, the back stretches in the Flexibility section (see page 76) may reduce the risk of a recurrence. Whatever the problem, if it is a genuine *injury* then:

STOP TRAINING – SEEK MEDICAL ADVICE

The remaining chapters in this book should help you understand the principles of physical conditioning and devise your own programme. Don't forget to use good goalsetting to help you stay motivated as you improve your fitness. Once you are fit your sailing will improve too.

2 Preparing for action ────────────

This chapter describes warming up and stretching both prior to training and on the water before racing. You can find some useful exercises at the end of the book.

Before you begin any kind of training you *must* warm up. You do this in two ways. First, by using your muscles in a relatively gentle way you generate heat so that they reach their ideal operating temperature. Second, by stretching you increase the mobility of your joints and the pliability of the muscle tissue surrounding them.

At the end of the training session you should also warm down so that your body returns to a state of rest gradually and has time to remove the waste products which have accumulated in its muscles. A less intensive warm-up, with sub-maximal stretches, can be used as a warm-down.

It is also a good idea to do some mental training at these times: both as preparation for the task ahead and by giving yourself an affirmation when you have completed it.

Raising the temperature

When muscles work, they generate heat. This heat is circulated by the cardiovascular system – better known as the heart and blood vessels – and is lost by the evaporation of sweat. However, most of the time our muscles are not working at their optimum temperature because the body diverts the heat to vital organs such as the brain.

Luckily, muscles have the capacity to warm themselves up. To do this they need oxygen to release energy from the fuels they contain. This is delivered by the blood supply, and gets into the blood in the first place from the lungs. This system of oxygen transport is known as the cardio-respiratory system. Ultimately it is the efficiency of this system which determines the capacity of working muscles to produce power.

The word 'aerobics' has become a generic term for the development, through training, of an efficient cardio-respiratory system. Such efficiency is known as aerobic endurance, and it is an essential foundation for other forms of training and for the maintenance of a healthy lifestyle. You need aerobic endurance, both to help warm up the body's muscles and to keep them working while you train or sail. If you doubt this, just consider what happens when you sail in medium to strong winds. Your heart-rate will usually be raised and your breathing will speed up. This indicates that energy is in demand and that your cardio-respiratory system is responding.

This in itself is a good enough reason for aerobic training – particularly if you are a boardsailor. Keelboat sailors have it easier, but the kind of fitness they need still has to be acquired through training, and you cannot train adequately unless you warm up first by doing aerobic exercise.

HOW OFTEN, HOW HARD?

Two or three sessions a week of the right kind of training will produce a real improvement in your aerobic endurance, but there are two important considerations. First, your heart rate needs to be raised significantly; second, it needs to be maintained at this high level for a reasonable duration.

A minimum length of time to exercise when *starting* a physical conditioning programme is 10-15 minutes; this enables the body to begin to adapt to the strains placed on it. Once you have reached a reasonable level of fitness, the minimum exercise time for developing aerobic endurance is at least half an hour.

Your heart rate is the key to efficient training, since it indicates the intensity of the exercise. It can be measured by taking your pulse, either in your wrist or neck, within 10 seconds of stopping the exercise, or – more

 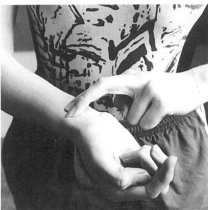 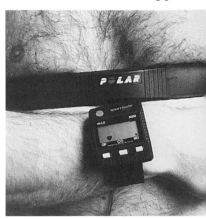

LEFT **You can take your pulse in your neck or in your wrist – but use your finger, not your thumb. Take a 15-second count and multiply the number by four to calculate the beats per minute.**
RIGHT **A heart-rate monitor will do the job for you.**

accurately – by using a heart-rate monitor. These are now widely available and relatively inexpensive.

Many people think that aerobic training should push your heart rate to the limit. This is not true; indeed training at such intensity could be dangerous. You should aim to achieve different heart rates during different types of training, and your age is an important factor (see Box 1 overleaf).

Improving your aerobic endurance
Although the duration of exercise is an important factor, this does not mean that training has to be monotonous. Almost any vigorous activity carried on for an extended period will help improve your aerobic endurance; in practice most people opt for running, for the simple reason that it is the most time-efficient. Cycling, either on or off the road, swimming or rowing are also good, but require equipment or facilities. One point is worth making about running: hard surfaces can play havoc with your body as you pound along, so you must invest in some proper running shoes.

You could also join a health club and take advantage of aerobic classes – particularly if you are younger. Training alone can

be demotivating and occasionally risky. Finally, don't forget that you can vary the kind of aerobic training you undertake; such 'cross training' can help make exercise both interesting and enjoyable. We describe this in more detail below.

TYPES OF AEROBIC TRAINING

There are three main types of training which can be included in an aerobic endurance programme, each with a number of variations. We have used running in these examples, but you could substitute any of the vigorous activities. Any of these types can be used and you can mix and match to keep your interest up. The three categories are long, continuous exercise; varied-pace training, sometimes called by its Swedish name, *fartlek*; and resistance work.

Long continuous exercise
This is the training base for many sports, and sailing is no exception. The greater the duration and number of runs you undertake, the greater the potential for improvement of the body systems. But beware of overdoing things, especially if you are starting to train after a lay-off. As with all training programmes progression is the key, so begin with small distances and low intensities of effort. You should soon note a lowering of your resting pulse rate – an indication that

your cardio-respiratory system is working more efficiently.

There are two kinds of basic running:

● Steady, easy running – long, slow distance work.

● Hard running – in which you start slowly and gradually increase speed.

Of these, the first is the one most commonly used by sailors. if you use the second, take care to stay inside your heart-rate range.

Varied-pace training, or fartlek

Under-used by sailors, this is a combination of steady, continuous running with burst of faster running or short sprinting. This forces the body to work anaerobically (without oxygen) in the fast stages and build up an oxygen debt which is repaid during the subsequent phase of easy running.

The term 'fartlek' means continuous running at various speeds. An example of a 30-minute fartlek session might be:

1 Five minutes easy running to warm up.

2 Two minutes hard running, followed by three minutes easy running (repeat three times).

3 Five minutes medium-hard running.

4 Five minutes easy running to cool down.

In any Fartlek session you exercise for a certain length of time, say 30 or 40 minutes, rather than running a certain distance.

Resistance work

This is a very useful technique, and you can use it to add interest to your training programme. Basically it combines running with lifting a heavy weight – yourself.

Two types are commonly used:

● Repeated hill running. Which means what it says!

● Aerobic trails. This involves combining running at varying speeds with short bouts of hard exercise. An example of an aerobic trail with five exercises might be:

1 Five minutes jog/easy running to warm up.

2 Thirty seconds of squat thrusts, then two minutes running at 50 per cent of maximum speed.

3 Thirty seconds doing press-ups (on the ground or against a wall), followed by two minutes alternating 100-metre fast running with 100-metre jogging.

4 Thirty seconds of hopping – 15 seconds on each leg – then two minutes running at half speed.

5 Thirty seconds running on the spot, starting slowly, increasing to very fast, then slowing down again; followed by two minutes alternating 150-metre sprints with 150 metre jogging.

6 Shuttle runs – say six times ten metres.

7 Two to three minutes of easy running to cool down.

On-the-water warm-ups

Sailors are notoriously poor at physically preparing for action. We compete in a cold, damp, draughty environment, sometimes miles from the shore, and once the start gun goes we expect our bodies to operate at maximum efficiency as we storm up the first beat. This is asking too much. After all, you wouldn't expect your car, after standing outside all night, to give you instant maximum efficiency, would you? Normally you allow time for the engine to warm up and reach its operating temperature. It is exactly the same with your body.

Indeed there is a very strong case for undertaking a warm-up before you even launch the boat. Many sailing injuries are suffered while launching and recovering boats, almost certainly because too much has been demanded from cold bodies.

Once out on the water there is often a long sail to the start, or long waiting periods. As a result the body begins to cool down, causing the muscles to stiffen up. So before the warning signal you should devote two or three minutes to:

● Raising your body temperature.

● Stretching the parts of your body that you will use in the race.

● Repeating the first part in case you have cooled off again.

Running or cycling are out of the question as ways of raising your temperature, but

1 TRAINING HEART RATES

Several members of the 1992 UK Olympic squad used heart-rate monitors as part of their training. Why? Because by accurately determining his training heart rate a competitor can monitor the intensity of the exercise, and develop his aerobic efficiency by maintaining his heart rate within upper and lower limits (target zones) for pre-set periods of time. The chart below shows average target zones for different age groups.

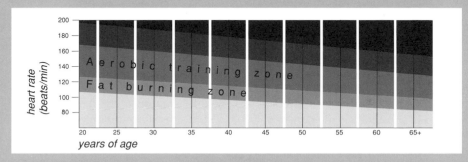

Ideally, you should work at between 65 and 85 per cent of your maximum heart rate. The higher the intensity of the exercise, the shorter its duration should be.

The fat burning zone is often of interest! However, fat burning does require exercise over a long period (45 minutes upwards) so 15 minutes of exercise at 50 per cent of maximum is unlikely to burn fat or do a great deal to develop your aerobic endurance. Nevertheless, if you are out of condition this may be all you can manage.

The beauty of monitoring your heart rate is that you can tell exactly how hard you really are working and how your body is adapting. A laboratory test will provide an accurate estimate of your maximum heart rate, but as most of us do not have access to these facilities a simple calculation can be used to find a reasonable value:

220 — current age = Maximum Heart Rate

The percentage of your maximum heart rate at which you should train depends to some extent upon your level of fitness, which depends in turn on your current racing and training schedule. You can simply read from the target range chart or use the following percentages as a guide:

- Racing only: 60-65% Max H.R.
- Racing, and training up to twice a week: up to 70% Max H.R.
- Racing and training regularly: up to 80% Max H.R.

For example, to find the target for a 30-year-old who is racing and training twice a week, first determine the maximum heart rate using the 220 — current age formula:

220 — 30 = 190 beats per minute (b.p.m.)

The level of fitness indicates training at 70 per cent of maximum heart rate, so:

Target = 190 x 70/100 = 133 b.p.m.

since your sailing clothing acts as insulation you can warm up quite quickly using mild exercise. Try gentle punching, becoming more vigorous; or gentle bicycling movements, either seated or lying on your back. Increase your rate of 'pedalling' to raise the temperature. Try elbow and arm circling, or doing press ups using the transom as a support. You could also run on the spot while in this position. These exercises – and any others you can think of – will help to prepare your body for the effort needed on the first beat.

STRETCHING – WHY DO IT?

Stretching is an important component of the warm-up and warm-down sequence. There are a number of very good reasons why you should always include stretching in your training, and use it before competing.

Stretching frees up the joints, so they have a bigger range of motion; this can help reduce the likelihood of an injury such as a muscle or joint strain. It can also make stiffness and soreness after exercise less likely, particularly if you have back problems. Less tangible – but equally important – are the improvements in your posture, and the way it helps you feel mentally and physically relaxed.

You should also use stretching exercises on their own, to increase the flexibility of the specific parts of your body that you will use in competition.

Types of stretching

There are three basic types of stretching, some of which are safer than others. You will find more information on safety in the stretching section at the back of the book. Choose a method that is right for you, in your circumstances.

Static stretching is where you stretch to the furthest comfortable position and hold the stretch for a few seconds. This is the safest form of stretching.

Ballistic stretching involves bouncing or bobbing movements. This is NOT RECOMMENDED as it can cause soreness and injury.

Passive stretching is where you remain relaxed while an outside force is applied, either mechanically or manually, to stretch your muscles. Often the stretch is applied by a partner. It is effective as long as it is used sensibly, under the control of a qualified, experienced instructor.

How to stretch

In your pre-exercise stretching you should aim to stretch the muscle groups you will be using during the coming training session, and hold the stretch for 8-10 seconds.

Once your exercise has ceased and your pulse rate is lowered, stretch the muscles you have just used in your exercise. Do not stretch them too hard, but hold the stretch for slightly longer, say 10-15 seconds.

For flexibility training you should choose a suitable stretching exercise but hold the stretch for at least 15 seconds, stretching 'deeper' as the tension eases.

What to stretch

Stretching exercises can be used for all the major muscle groups in your body. These include the neck and shoulders, arms, back, lateral trunk, abdomen, buttocks, hips and legs – particularly the hamstrings, which we have found are a source of problems for many top-flight sailors. Tight hamstrings restrict the movements of the pelvis and give the spine more work to do, often resulting in back problems.

You can find detailed descriptions of a range of stretching exercises which work on all these areas at the back of the book. Some of these will be suitable for use on the water, as well as on land.

3 Muscular fitness

Whenever you are hiking out, trimming sheets, moving out on the wire, connecting the spinnaker pole to the mast – in fact, whatever the task on a boat or board – you are doing some form of work involving your muscles. To perform these tasks well, you need muscle fitness. There are two elements to muscle fitness: muscular endurance and muscular strength. The kind of fitness *you* need depends on whether the activity is continuous or repetitive, or requires just one powerful effort. This chapter explains what this means in more detail and suggests a number of ways in which you can improve your own strength and endurance. Both of these are important, but your own muscular fitness will be shaped by the type of boat you sail.

MUSCULAR ENDURANCE

In many boats you have to use your muscles repeatedly, even continuously. Holding the mainsheet or hiking are two examples of actions which demand muscular endurance.

You can improve your muscular endurance by appropriate training using three main techniques.

Weight training Whether using weight machines, free weights or a combination, weight training is a popular form of training for sailors. Depending on how you carry out the exercises, weight training can be used to develop both endurance and strength in your muscles.

Circuit training This improves aerobic fitness, muscular strength and speed as well as muscular endurance. It can bring about many beneficial changes for all types of sailor, and can be carried out by young sailors so long as they take care to avoid heavy weights.

Simulators These can develop muscular endurance for specific actions. By asking a muscle to perform a movement in training over the same range, against the same resistance, the same number of times and at the speed required in competition, it is less likely to become fatigued by that same movement during competition.

If you don't have a simulator you can use a bit of imagination and create your own. For example, if you add things like mainsheet blocks or a hiking strap to a weight stack – even if only temporarily – you are likely to see the benefits of training more clearly than if you use standard equipment.

MUSCULAR STRENGTH

Put simply, muscular strength is the ability to apply force against resistance. Without strength in the appropriate muscles, you run the risk of being unable to perform a particular task or even injuring yourself.

This is particularly true on keelboats, because of the high loads involved in such tasks as winch grinding and making halyard and sheet adjustments. If you are a boardsailor you need strength in your arms for uphauling; hikers need strong legs to do the job, as well as strong arms for the mainsheet, while trapeze sailors need strength in their legs, arms and shoulders. There are tasks for which all sailors could benefit from extra strength, like lifting the boat off the trolley, righting a capsize and so on. In addition, strength can contribute to the performance of activities where muscular endurance is of prime importance. It follows that developing muscular strength should be a cornerstone of your physical conditioning programme.

The best way to acquire strength is through progressive resistance training, in which the muscles are required to work against increasing loads during successive workouts. This is usually achieved by training with weights, but other forms of resistance such as body weight, ropes or block systems can be used.

You should undertake a muscular endurance programme for four to six weeks before attempting strength training.

PLANNING A PROGRAMME

When you are planning a weight-based muscular fitness programme you need to take several factors into account. The two most important of these are the loads you will use and the number of repetitions you will make. Repetitions refer to the number of times an exercise is performed without stopping.

A further factor is the number of sets of repetitions. The number of sets and the length of the rests between them are important considerations.

Whether you are using circuit training or weights, the speed of a repetition should vary depending on the muscle group being used and the specific requirements of the action. If the movement is speeded up, for example, it may be less effective for developing controlled movements or the kind of style you should be aiming for. You should also maintain 'good form' to prevent injury.

You will need to rotate the exercise, simply because consecutive exercises on one area of your body produce rapid local fatigue. Make sure you arrange your exercises in an order which covers each body part in turn, and avoid doing the same exercise on consecutive days.

Strength and endurance training

In theory, if you want to acquire muscular strength you should use high loads, and a small number of repetitions; if you want to develop muscular endurance you should use relatively lower loads but do more repetitions. In practice, both endurance and strength can be improved by using quite a

---

EXERCISE ROTATION

arms → legs → abominals

back ← legs ← arms

---

1 THE PYRAMID SYSTEM

This technique is designed to build muscle strength and bulk. Relatively high loads are used but with few repetitions. It is an advanced form of weight training and should only be undertaken by experienced lifters. You will need expert help to consider things like the rests needed between sets, and how fast you should progress with the programme.

The first step is to determine the heaviest weight you can lift, just once. This is known as your one repetition maximum, or 1RM. The potential for injury and accident is obvious and you must not do this without assistance.

The programme is then based on a number of sets which take you closer and closer to your maximum weight. For example:

Set 1: 8 repeats @ 50% of 1RM

Set 2: 4 repeats @ 75% of 1RM

Set 3: 1 repeat @ 95% of 1RM

wide range of loads, repetitions and sets in combination, and our suggestions will cover both. A technique which is primarily designed to build muscle strength (and which can also be used to gain weight) is described in Box 1.

Making your training fit your needs

Don't build up strength and endurance mindlessly. Think carefully about which muscles you need to work on, because your needs for specific muscular strength and endurance will be shaped by the type of boat you sail. As a rule of thumb, the more the training exercise replicates the action needed in the boat, the greater the on-the-water benefit.

Recording progress

If you are to achieve maximum benefit from your training you need to adopt a structured approach. By recording your progress, you recognise the benefits more quickly.

Testing and recording may seem tedious, but after the first two sessions are completed you will find you have developed an effective self-monitoring and self-assessment system. You will have also developed more awareness about your body and its fitness. As with mental fitness, the more aware you become, the more control you can exert. You can read more about how this can be achieved for weight training in Box 2.

CIRCUIT TRAINING

Circuit training can be a very good way of developing muscular endurance. There are many variations on the theme, but most methods include:
● The use of body resistance and/or apparatus exercises.
● An arrangement of the exercises which permits progression from one station to the

---

2 KEEPING A RECORD OF YOUR PROGRESS

The first thing you must do in either strength or endurance weight training is find out where you start from. Then you will be able to monitor your muscle fitness improvements as they occur.

For muscle strength training, use your first session to find a weight you can just manage to lift five successive times; this is known as your five repetition maximum (5RM). For muscular endurance training, find your 8RM. Half this load is known as your training load for each type of training.

On the next session, find the number of repetitions you can perform in one minute, using this training load. Half this figure is your training repetition figure.

On subsequent sessions, use your training load to try to achieve three sets of training repetitions, with a maximum rest of one minute between sets. You may find this too difficult at first. If this is the case, just do as many repetitions as you can within each set before resting for the next. When you reach the target of three full sets, increase your training load by up to 5kg.

After four weeks, retest yourself and try to increase the maximum number of repetitions you can achieve in one minute using the current training load. Then record the new number of training repetitions (half the maximum).

You can use a sheet like the one overleaf to keep a record of your progress for each exercise. When you have achieved your target, start a new sheet.

other until all stations have been visited, the total comprising a circuit.
● A target time within which the circuit must be concluded or:
● A certain level of difficulty of exercises.

Ideally, circuits should be included during the development stage of your muscular fitness training. Many sports centres run public circuit training sessions which you can attend. However, with a bit of imagination you will find it easy to set up your own circuit at home.

Choosing exercises for your circuit

Just as with weight training, the more closely the exercises within the circuit represent the actions carried out on board your boat, then the greater the improvement in the appropriate muscles. Later in the book we have suggested a number of exercises which are appropriate for different types of sailor. You should pick eight or ten of these

for your own personal training circuit. So long as you are working on the part of your body which needs it, any of the several exercises which are appropriate for that area will be suitable.

One of the benefits of circuit training over weight training is that you can build in a lot of variety to keep yourself motivated. You can pick alternative exercises when you get bored and you can go around the circuit either way. It really doesn't matter where you start, so long as you complete the sequence in order.

Setting your work-rate

As with all forms of exercise, make sure you warm up properly before you start. Then decide whether you prefer using the number of circuits or the number of repetitions as a way of controlling the amount of effort you put into the training. You can use either; but whatever you use, the idea is to achieve a

TRAINING RECORD SHEET EXERCISE	8RM load	Training load	Max repeats in 1 minute	Target repeats	Target sets	Dates / Sets achieved							
					3								
					3								
					3								
					3								
					3								
					3								
					3								
					3								
					3								
					3								

steady progression in your training. So, as before, you need to employ some form of programme monitoring. Try these alternative ways of tackling circuit training and find one that works for you.

Method 1 The aim is to complete three circuits without resting. Start at your first exercise and work steadily through to the last exercise, then repeat the circuit twice more. Begin with 20 seconds on each exercise (which means that three circuits will take about 10 minutes to complete). When you can achieve this comfortably, increase the length of time on each exercise by 10 seconds. When you are happy with this add another 10 seconds so you are working for 40 seconds at each activity.

Method 2 Set a number of repetitions for each station, complete the circuit and note the time. On subsequent sessions try to shorten this time, until eventually you need to increase the number of repetitions.

Method 3 As with weight training, you can use a pyramid system (see Box 1). You will need to use the first session to find out the maximum number of repetitions you can perform in 60 or 90 seconds at each station. You can then use this information to design your personal pyramid.

It really doesn't matter which method you use, so long as you stick with it for a while to see how it is working.

USING A SIMULATOR

Few sailors would disagree that the best type of training for sailing is sailing. But by using a simulator you can create training regimes which are really quite close to the sort of training you get on the water.

This important fact has led to the widespread use of simulators. A good simulator can almost exactly duplicate the actions you need to perform on the boat, so the muscles you will use are specifically targeted.

That said, simulators are not entirely without drawbacks. There are two main problems. First, they are static, and do not simulate the actual movement of the boat on the water. Second, they can be relatively boring to use – certainly nothing like as exciting as actually sailing your boat!

Bearing these points in mind, any training schedule which you design should include both dynamic activity and interesting and varied routines. When you are hiking, for example, you rarely sit completely still. There is always some tensing and relaxing of the muscles, some shift of weight from leg to leg – as well as trunk movement to compensate for changes in wind and waves. In other words, continuous hiking is relatively dynamic, so you need to keep moving on your training bench if you want a reasonably accurate simulation of the real thing.

In addition, you engage in a great deal of other activity when you are afloat, such as constantly moving the tiller and mainsheet. So you should also try to include these sorts of movements when you are using your simulator.

When and how often?
A big advantage of simulator training is that it can be done at home, saving time. It also occupies less time than most general exercise sessions. But if you do use simulator training at home, don't forget to warm up and stretch your muscles before you start, and do a proper warm-down. Because the simulator trains specific muscle groups, you should reduce the amount of general training that you are doing, but do not stop it altogether. Simulator training develops muscular endurance, so it could replace, say, one circuit training session per week. Ideally you should do three or four sessions per week on your simulator.

We have suggested some ideas for simulator training at the back of the book. As with all muscular fitness training, these ideas are based on progressive exercises with varying repetitions.

4 You are what you eat ───────────

Coaches and sailors at international level are becoming increasingly aware of the importance of eating well to maintain health and improve sporting performance. For training, and in competition, it is important that you eat the correct balance of foods.

BASIC NUTRITION

In our diet we need a combination of proteins, fats and carbohydrates, as well as minerals, vitamins and water. Let's look at each of these in turn, in the context of competitive sailing.

Proteins
These provide amino acids, which are the body's building blocks. They are used both for growth and for the repair of body tissues, and play a vital role in every cell in the body. Many competitors imagine that they need to eat large amounts of protein to build up their muscles and increase their strength, but in fact a normal, healthy, balanced diet will do

this – in combination with a strength-training programme. You don't need to take protein or amino acid supplements either, so long as your dietary intake is good. There is no evidence that they help.

The main source of proteins in a normal diet are lean meat, fish, eggs, bread and pulses. It doesn't matter if you are a vegetarian or a carnivore, so long as you get moderate amounts of protein in your diet.

Fats
You also need fats in your diet. Fats are a very good source of energy since they have twice the calorific value of carbohydrates, but the body has great difficulty in breaking them down. It stores them instead, and as a result excess fat intake causes obesity and may lead to heart disease. Modern thinking is that a low-fat diet is better than a high-fat diet, and that your intake of saturated fats should be as low as possible.

Box 1 makes some suggestions about how you could change your diet for a healthier, low-fat one.

1 TEN WAYS TO REDUCE YOUR FAT INTAKE

Reduce the fat in your diet by:
1 Switching from frying to grilling.
2 Using olive oil when you have to fry.
3 Using semi-skimmed milk.
4 Eating out less – avoiding sauces and fried food in particular.
5 Using low-fat spread – thinly!
6 Using low-fat cheeses, such as Edam or Cottage cheese.
7 Cutting down (and preferably out) chips and crisps.
8 Eating lean meat, chicken without the skin or fish.
9 Eating boiled, jacket or mashed potatoes (but no butter!)
10 Reducing your consumption of pastry, pies, cakes and biscuits.

2 COMPLEX CARBOHYDRATES AND SUGARY FOODS

Complex carbohydrates are the foods that our bodies are adapted to use as fuel. They are relatively long-lasting sources of energy, and good for us in many ways. Good sources of complex carbohydrates include:
● Breakfast cereals (porridge, muesli and some wholegrain varieties)
● Bread (wholemeal and white).
● Pasta (include some wholewheat)
● Potatoes
● Rice (include some brown)
● Beans (baked, kidney or green), peas and lentils
● Root vegetables – fresh or frozen

Fibre or roughage, which is essential to maintain proper bowel function, is contained in all complex carbohydrates, as well as in figs, raisins, dates, nuts and prunes.

We can also use sugar as a source of energy. Refined sugar is found in a wide variety of products, such as:
● Chocolate bars, sweets, etc.
● Jams, marmalade
● Biscuits, cakes, puddings
● Sweetened or fruit yoghurts
● Fruit juices
These can give you a quick 'lift' but you should restrict your intake if you are serious about your diet.

Carbohydrates

Carbohydrates are built up from carbon, hydrogen and oxygen, and are the main source of energy in the diet. They come in two main forms. Simple carbohydrates are built up of simple molecules which are easily absorbed by the body. They include sugars such as sucrose, glucose and dextrose. Complex carbohydrates are built up of complex molecules which have to be broken down by the digestive system. An example is starch, which is composed of long chains of glucose molecules.

Many carbohydrate foods contain both sugars and starches as well as minerals and vitamins, but ideally you should keep the amount of simple carbohydrate in your diet to a minimum. Box 2 describes the sorts of foods which contain both simple and complex carbohydrates. You should bias your choice towards the complex ones, although the more refined, simple carbohydrates can be useful occasionally.

Minerals and vitamins

If you have a well-balanced diet additional minerals and vitamins should not be necessary. Vitamin pills are expensive and, in any case, cannot be stored in the body. Any excess is simply excreted.

A TRAINING AND RACING DIET

What you should be aiming for is a high-carbohydrate, low-fat diet that the body can turn into energy for muscular effort. This applies all year round, not just at regatta time; what you consume directly affects your ability to train and recover from training, just as much as your ability to perform well in competition.

If you think of food as a fuel, you will readily appreciate that you carry some around with you and use it up when you compete or train. So it is important to maintain your reserves when you are running at full throttle over a period of time, and the sooner you start refilling the tank, the better. Experience and research shows that if two or more hours elapse between finishing a hard race and eating, the energy levels the following day will not have recovered to the level of the first day. While the body may have sufficient reserves to perform effectively over a weekend, or even possibly a week of racing, serious energy problems can occur over a three- or four-week period.

So make sure you organise some way of replenishing your carbohydrate stores as soon as possible after a race. Many people take sandwiches on board, or use an 'energy drink'.

DRINKING

Fluid intake is very important, both when training and racing, especially in warm environments. Dehydration is a major cause of fatigue and can affect your judgement and ability to perform. You should aim to:

● Drink plenty of fluid before training or racing. You should aim to keep your urine 'pale and plentiful'.

● Keep sipping fluid during training and racing.

● Drink immediately after training or racing.

If you feel thirsty, it's too late - you are already dehydrated. The question is, what is the best sort of fluid to drink?

These days there are several 'energy drinks' and isotonic drinks on the market. Some are in powder form for adding to water and some are already made up. Should you use them?

If the requirement is purely rehydration and not energy or mineral replacement, then

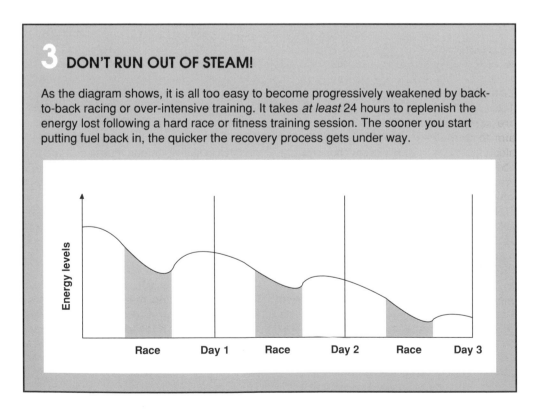

3 DON'T RUN OUT OF STEAM!

As the diagram shows, it is all too easy to become progressively weakened by back-to-back racing or over-intensive training. It takes *at least* 24 hours to replenish the energy lost following a hard race or fitness training session. The sooner you start putting fuel back in, the quicker the recovery process gets under way.

Energy levels

Race   Day 1   Race   Day 2   Race   Day 3

a dilute (five per cent) orange juice to water mix is fairly rapidly absorbed from the stomach (more quickly than plain water). But some 'sports' drinks claim to do more than this.

Isotonic drinks
This literally means 'in balance with the body's own fluids'. It is best to use these 20-40 minutes before exercising, or soon after the finish of a hard race or training session, especially in a hot climate.

Energy drinks
Glucose polymers are the most effective drinks for beginning the process of energy replacement. When made up in bottles they are the most flexible way to either maintain energy levels or aid rehydration. The ideal concentration depends on your body weight and requirements, but in general light winds or a hot day demand rehydration and a low concentration, whereas strong winds or a cold day demand energy replacement and a high concentration.

Alcohol
Alcohol cannot be metabolised by the muscles to provide energy. It can only be metabolised by the liver, at a very slow rate. The excess calories are stored as fat. If you are serious about your sailing, you should aim to drink very moderate quantities of alcohol. The negative effects (besides the obvious impairment of judgement and skill) are dehydration and appetite stimulation, which often upsets an otherwise balanced diet. Alcohol also adds too many 'empty' calories to the diet.

PLANNING YOUR NUTRITION

When you are competing, or undertaking intensive training, you will need to arrange your intake of food and drink to give you the best chance of performing at your peak. That means monitoring the amount of food you eat, as well as its type.

Your aim is to ensure that your energy levels are adequate and that you do not suffer from dehydration while performing. You also need to begin the process of energy replacement as soon as possible after the event. You may find these guidelines useful:
● Food intake during the two hours before exercise usually has a negative effect on performance. The control of blood glucose is affected, and muscle glycogen breakdown is increased – both of which lead to early fatigue. You may also suffer some physical discomfort. However, eating moderate amounts of carbohydrates three to four hours before exercise or racing is beneficial.
● During racing or exercise the carbohydrate reserves in the body are used up and dehydration can occur, especially in hot salty conditions. Wearing a wet suit or dry suit can speed up the process. So don't neglect fluid intake.
● Following racing or intense exercise, the body can take up to 36 hours to replenish its carbohydrate reserves, so consecutive days of hard exercise or training can lead to a decline in energy stores. Taking some form of carbohydrate immediately after racing or training greatly speeds up the replacement of reserves, accelerating recovery. So start the process as soon as you can.

A suggested nutrition plan for a race taking place at 1300 hours might be:
0800 Warm-up – jog/stretch.
0900 Breakfast – cereal, muesli or toast.
1115 Light meal – pasta.
1230 Start taking in fluid.
1300 Race (continue fluid intake).
1600 (or ASAP upon finishing) Sandwiches, a high-carbohydrate meal or a glucose polymer drink.
1900 Evening meal.

Competing abroad
Try to avoid eating meals in restaurants, because you lose control of your intake. Instead, organise self-catering accommodation, take staple foods with you and learn to cook three or four simple dishes based on pasta, rice or baked potatoes.

5 Recommended exercises

All the exercises described here have been categorised to help you to design a personal fitness programme to suit yourself and the boat you sail. Each exercise is illustrated by a photograph and accompanied by a description of how you should perform it.

Classification

The classification is of two kinds. First, each *exercise type* has been given a letter code:
F land-based stretching and flexibility exercises
FW on-the-water stretching
WT weight exercises
C circuit exercises

Second, each *type of sailing* has been categorised, as follows:
W Windsurfing
H Hiking
T Trapezing
K Keelboat crewing

To help you choose appropriate exercises for your own kind of sailing, you need only look for *your* letter code on the exercises. To make it even easier we have made suggestions for exercise programmes for each type of sailor. Each programme includes a range of exercise types which will develop the general and specific fitness you need. You may wish to substitute alternative exercises, but please make sure you cover all the body areas you will be using.

This chapter is divided into four sections: stretching, weight training, circuit training and simulator exercises. Stretching and flexibility exercises should *always* be part of your warm-up and warm-down routines, so *all* sailors should incorporate them into their training and preparation routines.

STRETCHING EXERCISES

These exercises fall into two categories: land-based, and those you can undertake on the water. The exercises cover the neck, shoulders, arms, back trunk, hips and buttocks, and legs.

You should select eight or ten exercises which will form your own stretching routine. It goes without saying that these should cover all the parts of your body to ensure that you are properly set up for subsequent muscular fitness training.

---

1 TEN SAFETY RULES WHEN STRETCHING

- Ensure the safety points discussed in Chapter 1, *Taking care of yourself*, are taken account of (see page 68).
- Warm up prior to stretching, and keep warm during the stretching session.
- Work on a suitable surface, such as a camping mat.
- Move slowly and smoothly into the stretch.
- Aim for good posture and stability.
- Breathe normally and freely.
- Do not strain or force a joint beyond its normal range of motion.
- Concentrate, and feel the stretch.
- Come out of each stretch as carefully as you went into it.
- Avoid pain.

Don't forget the rule of thumb about timing for these exercises:
● Warm-ups: hold for 8-10 seconds.
● Warm-downs: hold for 10-15 seconds.
● Flexibility: hold for at least 15 seconds and stretch 'deeper' as the tension eases.

Remember that these exercises are not about exertion; their job is to loosen you up, and improve your flexibility. Nevertheless, you must take precautions when undertaking any exercise, and Box 1 has some rules which apply to the exercises in this section.

NECK EXERCISES

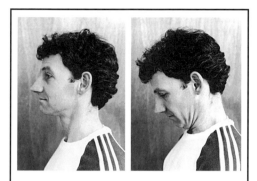

F1 Camel tuck.

F2 Neck side to side. Press head against hand.

SHOULDER EXERCISES

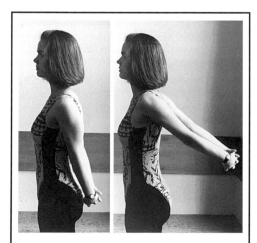

F3 Clasp hands together behind back and lift arms straight up behind you. Keep back as straight as possible.

F4 Clasp hands together above head, keeping elbows straight. Take hands behind head as far as they will go. Hold and repeat. Do not allow your trunk to sway back.

ARMS

F5 Hold one arm out in front of you with the palm facing away. Grasp these fingers with the other hand and gently pull them back towards you, keeping the elbow straight. Hold and repeat for the other arm.

F6 Sit or stand with one arm bent and raised above your head next to your ear, with your hand on your shoulder blade. Grasp elbow with opposite hand. Pull elbow towards the back of the head. Hold the stretch and relax.

BACK

F7 Kneel on all fours with toes facing backward. Contract your abdominals and round the back. Feel the stretch in your upper back and shoulders. Relax and return to the flat-back position.

F8 Sit with one leg bent on the floor and the other crossed over it. Inhale and twist your torso to one side until you feel a pleasant stretch. Hold and repeat on the other side.

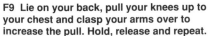

F9 Lie on your back, pull your knees up to your chest and clasp your arms over to increase the pull. Hold, release and repeat.

LATERAL TRUNK

F10 Sit upright on a hard chair. Turn to one side and place your hands on the back of the chair. Repeat on other side.

F11 Sit upright on the floor, fingers interlocked, hands behind head. Bend your upper torso to the side: try to touch your elbow on the floor outside your thigh. Relax and repeat on other side.

ABDOMEN, BUTTOCKS AND HIPS

F12 Stand with feet shoulder-width apart. step forward with one leg and sink down, bending leg gently until your hands touch the floor. Hold, return to standing and repeat.

F13 Lie on your back with one foot crossed over the other knee. Flex knee and push the other foot toward your face. Assist using hands interlocked behind knee.

LEGS

F14 Lie on one side. Grasp the toes of your upper leg and gently pull heel into buttock. Relax and repeat on other side.

F15 Lie on your back, raise one foot vertically, keeping it straight. Grasp calf or foot, pull gently to increase range of movement.

Stretches you can do on the water are obviously somewhat more limited. However, you may be able to include F6, the triceps stretch, and F14, the quadricep stretch. We suggest you also try the following, which can be done in a relatively confined space.

FW1 Gentle neck movements to increase mobility.

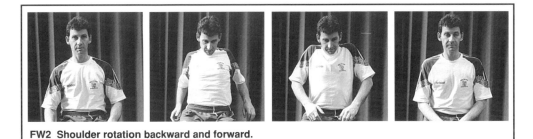

FW2 Shoulder rotation backward and forward.

FW3 Trunk twisting.

FW4 Buttocks and hips.

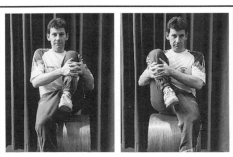

FW5 Lower back.

  **FW6 Lateral trunk.**

  **FW7 External rotators.**

  **FW8 Forearm flexors.**

  **FW9 Shoulder and upper back stretch.**

   **FW10 Lateral shoulder.**

WEIGHT TRAINING EXERCISES

One of the decisions you will need to make is whether to use free weights or weight machines. Both types of weight training equipment have their advocates and they have advantages and disadvantages for sailors. Even weight machines are of different types, among the most popular being the Nautilus type of isokinetic training equipment. In practice the choice of equipment is largely a matter of personal preference, although weight machines have the advantage that they can be modified by the addition of a sheet running through a block to simulate sailing actions.

Free weights must be used in the presence of helpers, and require a higher degree of skill in the execution of the exercises. They are generally used by more advanced weight trainers, or those looking for specific improvements in strength, but when used correctly they can produce good results.

WT7 Bench press. Lie face up with feet apart on the ground, or preferably on the bench. Push up from the chest until your arms are straight, and slowly lower. W H T K

WT8 Alternate dumbell press. As bench press, but using two separate dumbells. Raise one arm, lower, then raise the other. W H T K

WT9 Upright rowing. Stand with the bar at your waist and palms of hands facing down. Lift bar to chin and slowly lower. You could use dumbells or a shoulder-width grip. W H T

WT10 Seated rowing. Sit facing bar at shoulder height, arms extended. Grasp bar and pull arms back. W H T K

WT11 Bent-over rowing. Place one hand and a knee on bench. Keep back flat and look forward. Lift dumbell straight up from floor. Do not let arm lock out on release. Repeat with other arm. H T K

WT12 Dead lift. With your feet hip-width apart, take an overhand grip on the bar. Align knees with feet, keep back flat and backside higher than knees. Look forward and slightly down. Stand up, leading with shoulders and keeping the bar close to the body. Do not hyper-extend knees. Lower by flexing at knees and hips, with back straight. W H T K

WT13 Side bends. Holding dumbell, stand with feet shoulder-width apart and lean upper body away from the weight, keeping body in lateral plane. W H T K

WT14 Toe press. Adjust seat so you sit on the leg press machine with legs straight. Press toes forward and then return under control. W H T

WT15 Leg press. Adjust seat so legs are bent at right angles at the knees. Straighten legs. Lower weights slowly. W H T K

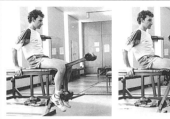

WT16 Leg extensions. Sit on bench, upright, ankles on the padded rollers. Straighten legs, lower 15 cm and straighten them again. H T K

WT17 Standing calf/heel raise. Adjust pads level with shoulder above armpits. Stand on platform, legs bent, take weight on shoulders. Stand up, heels off edge. Lift heels as high as you can, then lower below platform. W H T

WT18 Leg raise/ hip flex. Hang in the chair, legs straight below you, holding handles with back pressed into support. Raise knees as high as possible towards chest. Lower and repeat. H

WT19 Leg curls. Lie face down with backs of ankles on the padded rollers. Slowly bring rollers up to right angles, then lower them slowly. W H T K

WT20 Half squat. With feet shoulder-width apart, hold bar behind neck, resting on shoulders. Head up, shoulders back with overgrip. Keeping a flat, upright back, lower hips and bar by bending legs, pushing knees outward. Do not lower knees beyond 90 degrees to floor. Lift again by straightening legs and pressing hips forward. H T K

WT21 Dumbell grind. Adopt a comfortable stance and hold dumbell in front of body with both hands at a comfortable level. Rotate dumbell clockwise and anticlockwise. Six rotations equals one repetition. K

SUGGESTED WEIGHTS PROGRAMMES

Exercises marked ◆ should be alternated between sessions.

WINDSURFER
WT13 Side bends
WT17 Standing calf/heel raise
WT10 Seated rowing
WT15 Leg press
WT5 Lateral pull to waist
WT3/4 Wrist rolls/curls ◆
WT18 Leg raise / hip flex

HIKER
WT15 Leg press
WT14 Toe press
WT19 Leg curls
WT20 Half-squat
WT16 Leg extensions
WT3/4 Wrist rolls/curls ◆

TRAPEZER
WT12 Dead lift
WT2 Arm/bicep curls
WT15 Leg press
WT9 Upright rowing
WT16 Leg extensions
WT13 Side bends
WT17 Standing calf/heel raise

KEELBOAT CREW
WT12 Dead lift
WT5 Lateral pull to waist
WT15 Leg press
WT11 Bent-over rowing
WT16 Leg extensions
WT21 Dumbell grind
WT7 Bench press
WT19 Leg curls

CIRCUIT TRAINING EXERCISES

These are based on relatively simple activities that you can carry out with a minimum of equipment. You can do them in a gym, or at home. Pick about ten which will work on the parts of your body which need to become fitter. If you wish, you can simply use the set we suggest for the type of sailing you do.

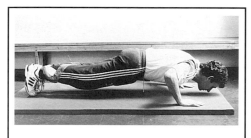

C1 Standard press-up. Keep a straight back. W H T K

C2 Press-up with feet on bench. A more difficult alternative. Keep a flat back. K

C3 Modified pull-up. With hands on bench or hands and knees on ground.

C4 Triceps dips. Lift yourself up, then gently down. T K

C5 Step-ups. Up on the bench, then down. W H T K

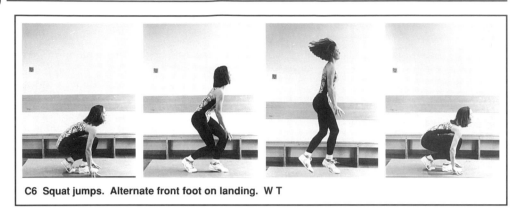

C6 Squat jumps. Alternate front foot on landing. W T

C7 Astride jumps. W H T K

C8 Squats. Knees not below 90 degrees.
W H T K

C9 Single leg squat thrusts. W H T

C10 Full squat thrusts. W H T

C11 Shuttle runs. W H T K

C12 Lunges. These must be slow and controlled. W H T K

C13 Bench jumps. W H T

C14 Bent-leg sit-up. Slow and controlled. W H T K

C15 Bent-leg sit-up with twist. Slow and controlled. W H

C16 90-degree sit-ups. Slow and controlled. T K

C17 Vertical leg sit-ups. Slow and controlled. T K

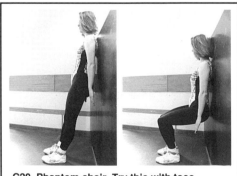

C18 Alternate leg sit-ups. H T K

C19 Vertical-leg sit-ups with alternate toe reach.. T K

C20 Phantom chair. Try this with toes raised. H T K

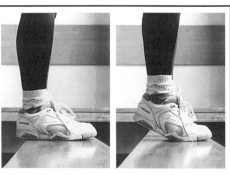

C21 Heel raise. Alternate feet on block. W T

C22 Grinder arms step-ups. Keep head down. K

SUGGESTED CIRCUITS

WINDSURFER CIRCUIT
C1 Standard press-ups
C19 Vertical leg sit-ups
C15 Bent leg sit-up with twist
C3 Modified pull-up
C8 Squat jumps, alternate front foot on landing
C22 Heel raise
C11 Shuttle runs
C13 Bench jumps, side to side

HIKER CIRCUIT
C11 Shuttle runs
C16 90-degree leg crunches
C20 Phantom chair, toes raised
C9 Single-leg squat thrust
C1 Standard press-ups
C7 Astride jumps
C18 Alternate-leg sit-ups
C5 Step-ups

TRAPEZING CIRCUIT
C3 Modified pull-ups
C10 Squat thrusts
C4 Triceps dips
C17 Vertical-leg sit-ups
C1 Standard press-ups
C8 Squats (no weight)
C11 Shuttle runs
C14 Bent-leg sit-ups

KEELBOAT CIRCUIT
C2 Press-ups with feet on bench
C11 Shuttle runs
C19 Vertical-leg sit-ups with alternate toe reach
C4 Triceps dips
C20 Phantom chair
C7 Astride jumps
C21 Grinder arm step-ups
C8 Squats (no weight)
C3 Modified pull-up
C5 Step-ups

SIMULATOR EXERCISES

We have suggested exercises which you can do on a hiking bench. Of course, if you connect a mainsheet to a rowing machine, you have another kind of simulator. You may even go so far as to build your own.

A simple hiking bench can be used to develop strength and endurance in those muscles which operate on the water – in the legs, arms and stomach. To make this approach to training as effective as possible, don't forget to make it as realistic as you can. So:

● Do not sit still. Twist from side to side, leading with each leg in turn.
● Move in and out occasionally to simulate gusts and lulls.
● Always use a good hiking posture, with bent legs and a convex back.
● Although the simulator should be built to mimic the shape of your boat, you should add padding at any bearing surfaces to avoid crushing nerves or blood vessels.

ABOVE **Always use good hiking posture, with bent legs and convex back (top). Hiking flat (bottom) will inevitably damage your back.**

Developing your programme

As with weight training the first session should be used to determine the training effort you will use on subsequent sessions.

Leg exercises

Hike for as long as you can in one go. Base your leg work on this time as shown below.

Arm exercises

Add a mainsheet block and sheet to both edges of your simulator, attached to shockcord at the rear of the bench. This simulates the mainsheet pull on both tacks. By altering the shockcord tension, the mainsheet load can be increased or decreased.

BELOW **A well-made hiking bench with toe strap, based on the gunwale profile of a 470.**

LEGS	Hiking period	Sets	Rest
Initial sessions	50% max	3 secs	45
Increase to:	50% max	5-8	60

ARMS	Repetitions	Sets	Rest
Initial sessions	15	3	alternate arms: no rest
Increase to:	20	5	as above
Then increase resistance:	15	3	as above

You should move the mainsheet about 25-40 cm on each pull. Ideally, the loading on the sheet from the shockcord should be

very close to that which you experience on the boat itself. However, you may find that, at first, you cannot achieve the number of repetitions we recommend. If this is the case, by all means slacken off the shock-cord a little. You can always increase it as your muscular fitness improves.

Stomach exercises

The hiking bench is an excellent way of developing your abdominal muscles, but you should take great care when doing these exercises that you do not let your back go lower than 45 degrees to the horizontal. Keep you head up, with your chin on your chest, as you lean back. This is quite an advanced technique, and young sailors should certainly have adult supervision while attempting it. This is especially true if the hiking bench mimics a boat where the sid-edeck is very narrow, such as the Optimist or Mirror, because there is some risk of knee damage.

You will have to determine your training load on the first session, or with the leg exercises. Find out how many sit-ups you can do in, say, 60 seconds. In subsequent sessions, you will use 50 per cent of this maximum with appropriate rests.

A set, at least initially, should consist of two groups of sit ups, each comprising 50 per cent max, separated by 30 seconds' rest. You should start with three such sets, with one minute's rest between sets. Later you will be able to increase the number of sets to five, and eventually retest yourself and set a new training target.

Also published by Fernhurst Books